Socialism and the New Life

Sheila Rowbotham
Jeffrey Weeks

# Socialism and the New Life
### The Personal and Sexual Politics of
### Edward Carpenter and Havelock Ellis

Pluto  Press

First published 1977 by Pluto Press Limited,
Unit 10 Spencer Court, 7 Chalcot Road, London NW1 8LH
Copyright © Pluto Press 1977
ISBN 0 904383 52 0 paperback
    0 904383 53 9 hardback
Cover design by Richard Hollis, GrR
Printed in Great Britain by The Camelot Press Limited,
Southampton

# Contents

## Acknowledgements

We owe thanks to a large number of people. The inspiration for the book came from a series of talks given to the Gay Culture Society at the London School of Economics in 1974. We must thank Philip Conn for asking us to give the papers in the first place, and the audiences who listened to us, for their comments and criticisms. Secondly, we owe a great deal to Bob Cant and Gloden Dallas, who travelled part of the road with us and read various drafts. A number of colleagues, friends and loved ones have given us helpful advice and much enthusiasm, especially: Paul Atkinson, Dilip Barua, Sue Bruley, Micky Burbidge, Shirley Bury, Val Clarke, Ruth First, Alastair Hatchett, Philip Jones, Dave Mason, Yoshiko Miyake, George Pearson, Stef Pixner, John Quaill, Marsha Rowe, Raphael Samuel, Ann Scott, Amanda Sebestyen, Vic Seidler, Angus Suttie, Edward and Dorothy Thompson, David Widgery, Graeme Woolaston. We also received friendly comments from Sheila's WEA classes, at Euston and in the Essex Road Women's Centre, and from History Workshop.

Mike Kidron and Richard Kuper of Pluto Press showed much patience and gave sound advice, and we are grateful for their encouragement.

We owe thanks to the copyright holders of the various works quoted here, especially the Society of Authors (for Havelock Ellis); to various libraries and owners of collections of papers for permission to use and quote from them, especially Sheffield City Libraries (for the Carpenter papers), the Brotherton Library, University of Leeds (for Alf Mattison's papers), John Rylands

University Library of Manchester (for the Sixsmith papers), King's College, Cambridge (for the Ashbee and Lowes Dickinson papers); Felicity Ashbee and the Victoria and Albert Museum (for the Ashbee Memoirs); and E.P.Thompson (for the Mattison Letter book); and to other libraries who helped us at various times, including the British Library, and the British Library of Political and Economic Science.

Finally, we must thank the typists who struggled with our unruly manuscript, including Jean Ali, Val Clarke, Eileen Pattison and Jane Bowden. Without them this book would never have seen the light.

## Introduction

This book is about two men who attempted to explore the inter-connections between the transformation of personal life and wider external radical social change in the late nineteenth and earlier twentieth centuries. Edward Carpenter (1844–1928) was a socialist pioneer, a poet fascinated by eastern religion, a penal reformer and advocate of a 'simpler life', a homosexual who wrote about homosexuality and ardently supported feminist aspirations. Havelock Ellis (1859–1939) was a sexual theorist, who greatly influenced liberal sexual ideas, but also an influential writer on literature, art, travel, philosophy and social policy, who formed his earliest political ideas in the small socialist groups of the 1880s. Writing about the life and work of Carpenter and Ellis we want to do more than discuss particular attempts at connecting the personal and political; we hope to raise wider questions about the socialist movement. A preoccupation with the position of women, with homosexuality and with sexual theory has been rare in labour history. Yet historical understanding of sexual relations is essential for any discussion of socialism as a 'new way of life'.

Past intensities wear thin with time and history has a way of obscuring what was obvious. Connections which were vital and living loosen with age and use. Taken for granted one moment, too evident perhaps to state or record, they are gone the next. The late Victorian world and its private passions remains now as faded photographs which set and limit our impressions. Yet the need to understand is compelling because the implications of the connections the two men were making have an obvious relevance.

In their effort to relate subjective experience to practical action for a more equal and democratic society they went far beyond a notion of politics which is only about parliament or elections or even about change in the ownership of production. They were preoccupied with sexual pleasure, with how to live communally, how to live equally without fear of authority, how to love one another in a loveless world, how to create beauty democratically in the midst of ugliness and competition.

They have been dismissed easily as cranks and visionaries, old photographs to be shuffled away. But this is to dismiss what was vital and living in the socialist tradition to which they belonged. Now that many of these concerns have re-surfaced in the socialist, feminist and gay liberation movements such a dismissal obscures how the concern to transform every aspect of life has been a recurring aspect of radical endeavour. Not that the past shape of such concerns can be excavated intact as a replica of our politics: this would be merely to substitute the present for the past and simply swallow our own tail. Our point is to uncover past intensities in order to distinguish what 'was' from what 'is'.

We are committed to this uncovering by our own involvement in socialism, sexual politics and feminism. We do not see these studies as presenting 'lessons' for now; we do see them as helping our understanding of our own predicament.

It is hard now to understand the hold in the Victorian period of the middle-class family, the authority of the father and husband or of an ideology which stressed wifely submission, rejected sexual pleasure and preached salvation through abstinence and thrift. This orderly universe of duty and earnest endeavour was precarious. Sinister dangers lurked in the beyond, a confused and dreadful nightmare of a world without God, of class conflict, revolution, disease, sexual degradation and criminality. These perils were all the more terrifying because they could not be spoken about or clearly distinguished, a miasma of horror and moral terror. The Victorian poet and writer, J.A.Symonds, believed as a little boy of seven that the devil lived near the doormat and screamed at night about imaginary sins. In a recurrent nightmare he saw retribution:

> I dreamed that we were all seated in our well-lit drawing-room, when the door opened of itself, just enough to admit a little finger. The finger, disconnected from any hand, crept slowly into the room, and moved through the air, crooking its joints and beckoning. No one saw it but myself. What was the horror that would happen if it should touch me or any present, I never discovered, for I always woke before the catastrophe occurred.[1]

Fear of retribution dissolved into doubt and insecurity, the universe became a remorseless steam-engine leaving human beings stranded and isolated. There was a real basis to this fear and dread. Nineteenth-century capitalism had torn up an agricultural society from its roots, manufactured machines on an unprecedented scale, mushroomed cities, concentrated the poor in such numbers that the concept of the 'masses' could appear, and brought into being a new class with little to pawn but their chains. The notion of classes as opposed to estates or stations came out of this new reality. The contrast between the class who sold their labour power and the employing class was stark and clear. Other forms of social relationships also changed as middle-class women passed out of production. Powerless, they became part of the decor of privilege. Middle-class masculine thinking sought elaborate justification for the subordination of the working class and of women. A notion of masculinity adequate to the task had to be mustered, the stiff upper lip, be-whiskered chin and muscular Christianity became the anatomic destiny of young Victorian males in the middle years of the century. This was the stuff of empire building.

When it came, resistance to religion, to the family, to women's subordination, to rigid sexual attitudes and personal behaviour and to class inequality, was passionate and intense, for the hold of the values of the middle class was very strong, haunting the dreams of childhood. Samuel Butler's *The Way of All Flesh* was finished in the 1880s but could not become popular until early in the twentieth century because of its vehemence against religion, the fear of fathers, the middle-class family, the gloom of Sundays and its portrayal of hypocrisy, narrowness and sanctimonious morality. In the 1890s Thomas Hardy's *Jude the Obscure* caused a storm of vitriolic protest because it challenged not only class but conventional sexual attitudes, and Hardy never wrote another novel.

The mid-Victorian certainty they attacked had never been completely secure. Even in the relatively prosperous years when progress was assumed to be natural, some of the old heresies from the early turbulent and insurrectionary years of the century trembled still. The trade unions, apparently placated, could still suddenly erupt. Free thinkers like George Jacob Holyoake and Charles Bradlaugh were prepared to meet churchmen in open controversy while the secularist movement made its own converts. German biblical criticism and Darwin's theory of evolution in the 1860s could trouble the intelligentsia into unbelief. Though the Chartist movement died and Owenite hopes of a new moral world grew faint, men and women involved in these early movements left a legacy of resistance. Some of these old-timers went into other radical causes, supporting foreign fighters for national freedom like Garibaldi and Mazzini and the Irish, or campaigning at home for the extension of the franchise, land nationalisation and republicanism. Their children inherited a tradition of dissent. On the extreme fringe of the radical left the vision of revolution never completely disappeared. In the 1860s and '70s working in the First International, in the radical clubs and in secularist organisations and in the groups formed for the vote or land nationalisation there were still those 'dreamers of dreams' biding their time until 'the kings of the nation' would be 'the scorned of the scorners of yesterday'.[2]

But this connecting vision remained submerged and until the late 1870s the pattern of single-issue campaigns and specific causes continued. Without the utopian consciousness of the early part of the century that looked to the transformation of all social relations, without a movement which sought to abolish hierarchies of class and skill, the radical strands became separated and thus changed. The early radicalism of the Owenites, for example, had carried a challenge to the total sexual division of labour and had contained the possibility of conceiving a new relationship of the body to nature, not bound by religious guilt. Some of them had seen that the specific material predicament of women required that sexual relationships and the structure of the family must change, so that women could realise sexual pleasure and exercise control over procreation.[3]

The middle-class feminist movement which developed in the second half of the century appears to have been wary of such connections, concentrating on securing property and some independence for married women, or improving education and the conditions of employment. Ironically the movement which raised the explosive issue of women's control over their own bodies was Josephine Butler's campaign against the Contagious Diseases Acts in the early 1870s. These Acts had been passed in the 1860s in an effort to protect the troops from VD. In certain garrison towns women could be stopped by the police on suspicion of prostitution and had to submit to examination for venereal disease or appear before a magistrate. Butler and her supporters produced a *Women's Manifesto* objecting to the Acts as an example of the double standard of sexual morality which punished women and not men, as a violation of the rights of women (and it was largely working-class women who were picked up and examined) over their own person, and morally opposing the official sanction to vice which they thought the internal examination of women gave. But the issue of a woman's rights over her own body became indistinguishable from the call for social purity in this kind of feminism. This tendency was reinforced by rescue work and the moral shock with which the middle-class reformers encountered, amidst poverty and overcrowding, the complexities and ambiguities of working-class family patterns as well as actual prostitution.[4]

In the late nineteenth century the idea of controlling births was presented, not as a feminist concern for sexual pleasure and autonomy, but as a Malthusian attempt to limit the numbers of the poor in order to prevent hardship. When a Bristol bookseller was given two years' hard labour in 1876 for publishing Knowlton's *Fruits of Philosophy* Charles Bradlaugh and Annie Besant, both secularists, took up the case as an issue of free speech. They saw birth control as 'a path from poverty for the poor'. But despite their limited aims, their conservative opponents saw birth control as sin's defiance of Providence and a rallying cry for hedonism among the outcast poor – a more extreme heresy than the radical middle-class Malthusian terror of a numerous poor. Sexuality was an explosive issue, so that even moderate reforming efforts could raise a torrent of criticism, controversy and violent reaction.

After the onset of the Great Depression in the mid 1870s a new awareness of the interconnectedness between the various radical causes began to develop. With Britain no longer economically supreme, there was a flagging of confidence among the upper classes. The Liberal Party, traditionally the party of reform, faced a new working-class electorate demanding concessions at one side and the rich landowners who maintained the party resisting them at the other. Disillusionment with liberalism was a slow affair and there were regional variations in the patterns of attachment and rejection. Dissatisfaction with the machinations of the local liberal establishment could combine with opposition to the Liberals' policy in Ireland. Concern about an extension of free education, militancy against liberal employers could bring a working-class radical to socialism. Some socialists came out of the secularist movement – despite the hostility of Bradlaugh to socialism. Others left religious groupings – for though it was possible for Christians to be socialists, the Church often seemed to be established on the side of respectability and privilege.

Among many of the young middle class in the 1880s, there grew a profound unease about their position of privilege, about the morality of a system which brought the unemployment and poverty which their earnest social enquiry uncovered, which banned the unemployed from demonstrating and sold girl children into prostitution. Some of these middle-class reformers tried to overcome inequality and exploitation by living in Settlements, hoping that personal contact would assuage class bitterness, and that detailed investigation of housing, poverty, work, unemployment would suggest the means of reform. The sheer proximity to the poor overwhelmed some of these settlers; others saw themselves in imperial and evangelical metaphors as colonisers, maintaining outposts and missions. Some observed their predicament wryly. One young man in business at the Toynbee Hall Settlement commented 'we shear the lambs all day and temper the wind at night'. A few moved beyond the Settlements to socialism or to active support of workers on strike. Charles Ashbee, a young architect who was at Toynbee Hall in the mid 1880s, became impatient with the work of the Settlement, flirted with socialism, drew back but went off to form a Guild and School of Handicraft. Influenced by Morris he wanted to integrate art with craftsmanship, thinking it better to design trade-union banners than to hang in the Royal Academy. Unlike Morris, though, he saw a revival of craft skill as a substitute for social revolution and earned Morris's hearty contempt for his pains.

The Guild and School of Handicraft was part of a wider cultural movement in reaction to every aspect of Victorian life. This involved not only a new and democratic aesthetic but an attempt to discover a new way of living. In the 1880s the boundaries between this moral, aesthetic and political revolt were still fluid. Members of the Progressive Association in 1882 included radicals and marxist social democrats for example and the Association saw the moral awakening which they sought as inseparable from political and social democrats for example, and the Association saw the moral many ways the advanced and earnest radicalism of the Russian intelligentsia. The later split between the Fabians and those who were more concerned about the 'new life' (and who continued in the Fellowship of the New Life) was amicable and never rigid in the 1880s. Havelock Ellis and Edward Carpenter were both members of the Fellowship, though the emphasis of their concerns differed. Ellis was interested in developing an understanding of sexual psychology while Carpenter was more of a populariser of sexual theory, preoccupied with the relationship of personal questions with the socialist movement, but both saw themselves as conscious path-makers.

Although H.M.Hyndman, the leader of the first marxist organisation in Britain, the Social Democratic Federation, appears to have been completely dismissive of feminism, sexual politics and concern for the quality of existence, the SDF was never simply the creature of one man. It included old Owenites and Chartists, exiles from the European revolutionary movement, land nationalisers, secularists. Theoretically the origins of English marxism may have been limited and narrow but culturally they came from a rich and varied tradition. When William Morris and other members of the Federation broke away to found the Socialist League they formed a group which emphasised cultural change and consciousness more than the SDF. But the League collapsed in the early 1890s with the Morris tendency defeated by anarchist-communism.

With the creation of the Independent Labour Party in 1893 there was an important shift in the theoretical preoccupation of British socialism. Revolutionary socialists and anarchists in the 1880s focused their debates on issues of organisation, on the degree of centralisation, the nature of leadership, on how far socialists should support particular reforms, or work in trade unions to improve immediate conditions, or participate in parliamentary elections or campaign for state intervention. The ILP from the first firmly accepted the need to get Labour candidates into parliament and was later to be part of the Labour Representation Committee, the modern Labour Party in embryo. In the 1900s the leaders of the ILP were concerned to present a 'reasonable' socialism and anxious to forget their links with revolutionary socialism. Nonetheless the local organisation of the ILP was often created by people who had been in the SDF or the Socialist League and, at a branch level, the old utopian concerns about the 'new life' persisted. The patterns of activity were similar: the importance of the club, of fellowship, the outdoor 'missionary' work, poems, songs, the belief that you had to have socialism inside you. The idea of socialism as a new form of community continued. To become a socialist was still often seen as becoming a different kind of person. But these utopian preoccupations became increasingly divorced from the function of sending Labour men to parliament. Socialism and the new life were indefinitely postponed, the time was never somehow quite right. The faithful waited for socialism to be granted from on high.

In opposition to this parliamentary socialism, ideas of direct action, of learning through doing rather than through words, resurfaced in the socialist movement in the 1900s. While ILP members worked locally in the trade-union movement and in community struggles, the young revolutionary syndicalists after 1910 were dismissive both of parliament and the official trade unions, searching for a direct democracy of work-place organisation. Although the context had changed it was a politics which could have been recognised by members of the Socialist League, and Carpenter was able to support the syndicalists.

Many questions remain obscure about the early socialist movement and about the differences between local activists and the leaders at the centre. A detailed study of the attitudes of these groups to the position of women, to the family, and to sexual politics is yet to be written. We do not know much about the role of women in the groups or the effect of an autonomous feminist movement on socialism after Mrs Pankhurst formed the Women's Social and Political Union in 1903.

The question is complicated by the fear of sexual issues entertained by the prominent leaders of the feminist movement. Many feminists argued that women had suffered so much from men's sexual desires both physically and psychologically that the aim should be to make men as spiritual as women had been forced to become by Victorian morality. So there was quite a clear division between advocates of birth control like Annie Besant and sexual radicals like Carpenter and Ellis on the one hand, and feminists like Millicent Fawcett on the other. The leaders of the more militant WSPU in the 1900s were equally suspicious of sexual radicalism. Christabel Pankhurst was prepared to use direct action but she had no sympathy for a growing current in the feminist movement which was asserting active female sexuality and discussing demands which related to the biological situation of women as women. The dissidents could be found grouped round the journal *The Freewoman* before 1914 and as advocates of the 'new feminism' demanding birth control, abortion, family allowances, better conditions for maternity in the 1920s.

Certainly from the 1880s there were women in the socialist movement who were aware of many aspects of women's oppression. Olive Schreiner, for instance, a South African novelist and feminist, or Eleanor Marx (Karl's daughter) who helped to organise the Gas Workers' Union, one of the new unions in which women had an equal status with men. When Eleanor Marx and Edward Aveling discussed Bebel, the German socialist's book *Women in the Past, Present and Future*, they criticised contemporary feminism not only for being middle-class – a condition Marx and Aveling admitted was shared by English socialism – but also for being within the limits of the society of today. The exception they noted was the agitation against the Contagious Diseases Acts which included working-class women and also touched women in their sex relations. Marx and Aveling were opposed not only to the power of the man over the women in marriage, the double standard of sexual morality, but also to the suppression of female sexuality. 'How is it that our sisters bear upon their brows this stamp of lost instincts, stifled affections, a nature in part murdered?' They shared the faith of early sexual radicalism that education could create better sexual relations. Like Olive Schreiner they opposed 'false shame and false secrecy' and believed that only when men and women 'striving after purity, discuss the sexual question in all its bearings, as free human beings, looking frankly into each other's faces' would there be any hope of a solution to the sexual question.[5]

Within the Socialist League the anarchist-communist wing seems to have been very much concerned with the structure of the family and sexual freedom though often in an abstract and male-defined way. They called upon anarchists to live out the new sexual relations regardless of the consequence. Opposition to marriage went with opposition to the state. An article in *The Sheffield Anarchist* in July 1891 presented a more developed statement. It was critical of the family for creating 'egoism' but was aware of its role also in defending people against the external ravages of the cash-nexus. The article was aware of the woman's labour in the family. 'If we should try to measure the value of the work done for the family by the mother, after the rules of political economy, the price would not be estimated.' The Sheffield anarchists were against the indissolubility of marriage as 'contrary to human nature' for 'we do not always live in the same way; our sentiments change or grow more perfect'.[6] The anarchists in the 1890s, despite persecution, kept this tradition alive and did live in free unions, the young women being proud of their dignity as free women.

As the socialist movement changed in the 1890s and 1900s, women continued to be prominent as speakers and organisers. Katharine St John Conway, Enid Stacy and Carolyn Martyn were all well-known and respected. There was still an awareness of the woman question. But equally there was an increasing tendency among socialists to see sexual change as an outcome of the economic re-organisation of society and to stress the positive role of the family as a defence against wage labour and capitalism. Many socialists who would recognise personal and cultural change as being very important were not prepared to admit the importance of sexuality. The assertion of the need to express sexual life which had appeared briefly in the revolutionary groups of the 1880s seems to be submerged again in the more gradual day to day struggles of the 1890s. Nonetheless local studies of the socialist movement might find a quite different reality.

The emergence of a more militant feminism with an autonomous organisational existence undoubtedly made a profound impact on the socialist movement. Hannah Mitchell, a working-class suffragette and socialist, describes the ambiguous and uneasy attitude of socialists towards feminism in her autobiography *The Hard Way Up*. The feminism of the 1900s was much wider than the vote and brought up again all kinds of questions about the relations between the sexes. This time it was not just the woman question, or the origin of the family in abstract but an opposition, both political and cultural, to every aspect of patriarchal hegemony. Attitudes hardened when the vote was not granted and feminists were divided both on the question of sexuality and on their class allegiance. The complex details of the socialist movement's response remain unknown. But we can outline the more obvious from the open opposition of a Hyndman in the SDF or a Bruce Glasier in the ILP, through the socialist women's cautious attempt at co-option by forming their own non-feminist organisation, to a Hannah Mitchell torn in her loyalty between a socialist movement which denied feminism, and a feminist movement which dismissed socialism, through to the outright anti-socialism of Christabel Pankhurst. The local reality presents a situation of women moving between feminism and socialism, not of the two clearly distinct movements which study of the organisational and political centres would indicate.[7]

If our present knowledge of the connection between socialism, sexual politics and feminism is limited, the history of the socialists' attitudes to male homosexuality and lesbianism is even more obscure both at the level of theory and of practice. Implicit within the most developed marxist statement on the family in this period, Engels' *Origin of the Family, Private Property and the State*, published in 1884, there are assumptions which not only influenced socialists' views of the sexual position of women but also the approach to sex between members of the same sex.[8] Engels' work begins with the essential pre-condition for a marxist analysis, the assumption that the sexual division of labour between men and women, and the historical supremacy of men over women, has a material base, is rooted in the mode of production. He then makes a second assumption: that the relationship he sees in the bourgeois family, with the male's supremacy based on his economic desire to ensure uncontested inheritance of his property, can be pushed back to the origins of class society. The overthrow of mother right and the growth of a social surplus controlled by men coincided with the 'world historic defeat of the female sex'. Whatever the historical validity of this, a logical deduction follows from it: that only on the basis of women's full re-introduction into social labour on equal terms with men will their liberation be achieved.

'The predominance of the man in marriage', Engels writes, 'is simply a consequence of his economic predominance and will vanish with it automatically.'[9] 'Automatically': behind this simple word are a number of assumptions which have persisted throughout marxist tradition.

Firstly, there is a clear assumption of the 'natural' biological basis of social roles. The sexual division of labour between men and women – with the women primarily responsible for child care – is not questioned. It only assumes oppressive qualities, we must understand from Engels, with the development of private property, and he seems to believe that under socialism the family will embody a traditional division of labour, even though many of the family's previous functions will be socialised.

Secondly, as a corollary of this, there is an inevitable bias towards heterosexuality. Marx and Engels inherited from the utopian socialists a classically romantic belief in the all-embracing nature of true love between men and women:

our sex love has a degree of intensity and duration which make both lovers feel that non-possession and separation are a great, if not the greatest calamity: to possess one another they risk high stakes, even life itself.

This sex love has been distorted by commodity production, but will flourish on a higher plane under socialism so that 'monogamy, instead of collapsing, [will] at last become a reality'.[10] Homosexuality is consequently abhorred, its expression seen as 'gross, unnatural vices'. Its manifestations are seen as symptoms of the failure of sex love and the degradation of women, so that, for example, in ancient Greece:

this degradation of women was avenged on the men and degraded them also, till they fell into the abominable practice of sodomy and degraded alike their gods and themselves with the myth of Ganymede.[11]

It would have been extraordinary in the early 1880s if Engels had thought otherwise, given the universal ignorance concerning homosexuality. It reveals, however, a failure to explore the social and historical determinants of sexual and emotional behaviour and character which underlines another key assumption.

Engels seemed to believe that sexual oppression can be directly deduced from economic exploitation, and without which it would disappear. As a result his outline of the family is bare and external, bones without flesh. He assumes that the 'personal' is natural and given, and that once the constraints of a society dominated by the pursuit of profit are removed private life would spontaneously adjust itself to a higher stage of civilisation. There is no concept of the need for conscious struggle to transform inter-personal relations as part of the transformations necessary for the construction of a socialist society.

Within the socialist movements of the Second International (1889 to about 1914) Engels' work was treated not as the starting point but as the last word. The key to women's emancipation was seen as entry into the work force, so that the women's struggle was related directly to the class struggle. Women's domestic labour was left unanalysed, as was the nature of 'personal' life and particularly female sexuality.

The late nineteenth century saw the consolidation of the theories about sexuality and personality which have dominated twentieth-century thought. In the first place, these stemmed from the post-Darwinian theories of evolution. The possibilities of biological adaptation which these suggested allowed certain concepts which had long been present in capitalist social theory to be put on an apparently 'scientific' footing. A good example of these is the notion of 'degeneration'. Thus we see the conceptualisation of the 'unemployed' from the 1880s in terms of a class of unemployables, the 'residuum', incapacitated from the struggle for life by their biological failings.[12] The division that the Webbs were to use in the 1900s between the 'deserving' and the 'undeserving' poor was very much in this tradition. Similarly in the 1880s and '90s we see old concepts decked out in new biological colours: of criminals being destined for their fate by the shape of their skulls or homosexuals for theirs by 'hereditary taint'. The sharpening division of labour within the working-class family, the increasing division between work and home, was provided with a biological justification: women were home-minders and child-bearers, destined by their whole biological evolution to be mothers of the race.

Socialist theorists were not immune from these trends. Carpenter and Ellis, in particular, were to work very much within existing concepts of gender roles: their implicit aim was to humanise rather than revolutionise social relations. Later, Stella Browne and other new feminists were to accept this and were not properly able to question the division of labour between the sexes. This is the most severe limitation of their work, and allowed the quiet absorption of many of their ideas into the mainstream of bourgeois thought by the 1930s.

Nevertheless, the questions raised by these pioneers are still significant. Even though their efforts were not by and large successful or long lasting, they touched on many vital connections which remain unresolved. The political implications of women's control over their bodies; the separation of sexual pleasure from procreation; the significance of homosexual love, of free unions, of changed ways of life and the relationship of all these to the labour and socialist movements, these are issues which, long ignored, are now again being discussed on the left.

### References

1. Horatio Brown, *Life of J. A. Symonds*, pp.7–8, quoted in Walter E.Houghton, *The Victorian Frame of Mind*, New Haven, Yale University Press 1957, p.63.

2. J.B.Leno, *The Aftermath*, London 1892, p.35, quoted in Stan Shipley, *Club Life and Socialism in Mid-Victorian London*, Ruskin College Oxford, History Workshop Pamphlets, No. 5.

3. See Barbara Taylor's forthcoming Sussex D.Phil. thesis for a detailed discussion of Owenite socialist feminism.

4. For a discussion of the attitudes of and towards working-class women, see Judith R.Walkowitz and Daniel J.Walkowitz, '"We are not beasts of the Field." Prostitution and the Poor in Plymouth and Southampton Under the Contagious Diseases Acts', *Feminist Studies*, vol. 1, Nos. 3–4, Winter/Spring 1973, pp.73–106.

**5.** Edward Aveling and Eleanor Marx, *The Woman Question*, London, S. Sonnenschein & Co. 1886, pp.1–12.

**6.** 'Woman and the Family', *The Sheffield Anarchist*, 19 July 1891.

**7.** For an account of some aspects of the relationship between socialism and feminism, see Sheila Rowbotham, *Hidden from History*, London, Pluto Press 1973, and *A New World for Women: Stella Browne, Socialist Feminist*, London, Pluto Press 1977. See also Sheila Rowbotham, 'Florence Exten-Hann, Socialist and Feminist', *Red Rag*, No. 5; Sheila Rowbotham's interview with Lilian Wolfe 'She Lived her Politics', *Wild Cat*, March 1975; and Nicholas Walter's obituary of Lilian Wolfe, *Freedom*, 24 May 1974.

**8.** See F.Engels, *Origins of the Family, Private Property and the State*, ed. Eleanor Burke Leacock, London, Lawrence and Wishart 1972, p.145. The section that follows is based on Jeffrey Weeks, 'Where Engels Feared to Tread', *Gay Left*, No. 1, Autumn 1975.

**9.** F.Engels, *Origins*, p.145.

**10.** *ibid.*, p.140.

**11.** *ibid.*, p.128.

**12.** For a discussion of this theme, see Gareth Stedman Jones, *Outcast London*, Oxford, Clarendon Press 1971.

Part 1
# Edward Carpenter: Prophet of the New Life
by Sheila Rowbotham

*Edward Carpenter*

Part 1

# Edward Carpenter: Prophet of the New Life
by Sheila Rowbotham

## Childhood and Cambridge

In his autobiography, *My Days and Dreams*, Edward Carpenter included an appendix written in 1914 in reply to a congratulatory letter from his friends on his seventieth birthday. In it he said that if he had had an effect on society it was because he was born when the commercial era was at its height and the suffering which that had caused him had forced a very intense opposition. The range of his criticisms indicates the extent of the changes he wanted. He saw the 'Victorian Age' as

a period in which not only commercialism in public life, but cant in religion, pure materialism in science, futility in social conventions, the worship of stocks and shares, the starving of the human heart, the denial of the human body and its needs, the huddling concealment of the body in clothes, the 'impure hush' on matters of sex, class-division, contempt of manual labour, and the cruel barring of women from every natural and useful expression of their lives, were carried to an extremity of folly difficult for us now to realise.[1]

He was still unable explicitly to list among his accusations the suppression of love between men, which was in his own life the most important aspect of that 'starving of the human heart'. He could only trust that the closest among his friends would understand.

His origins were conventional enough. He was born in 1844 into a comfortable upper-middle-class English family, his father was an ex-naval officer who had become a lawyer, and the family's fortunes were buttressed by substantial investments in British and

American railway companies. His father, Charles Carpenter, was very much of the material world the Victorians had made, worrying about his investments. But the elder Carpenter had been stimulated by middle-class radical ideas of utilitarianism in his youth and then like the troubled and earnest son of utilitarianism, John Stuart Mill, had wondered if utility quite encompassed the soul. However, he was not prepared to extend the utilitarian principle of the greatest happiness of the greatest number beyond the confines of the middle class. He settled instead for a comfortable compromise in a mystical Broad Church Anglicanism – the decent and reasonable version of Christianity that was so excellently suited to political liberalism. Charles Carpenter bequeathed its broadness absent-mindedly to his son along with his anxiety and his conscience – though Edward was to travel with his father's legacy into strange places. Edward's parents were kind, but true to the conventions of the times they distanced themselves from the children: 'we early learned to suppress and control emotion and to fight our own battles alone'.[2] Already in his teens he felt unhappy:

I did not know where I was. I had no certain tidings of any other feasible state of society than that which loafed along the Brighton parade or tittle-tattled in drawing-rooms. I only knew I hated my surroundings. I even sometimes out of the midst of that absurd life, looked with envy I remember on the men with pick and shovel in the roadway and wished to join in their labour; but between of course was a great and impassable gulf fixed, and before I could cross that I had to pass through many stages. I only remember how the tension and pressure of those years grew and increased as it might do in an old boiler when the steam ports are closed and the safety valve shut down.[3]

In his mother's eyes he saw the 'look of a prisoner'.[4] She faded into the role of self-sacrificing service which pressed the life out of so many Victorian women of the middle class. Watching the same pressures on his sisters, Carpenter began to question the limpid future respectability offered to women.

The life, and with it the character of the ordinary 'young lady' of that period, and of the sixties generally, was tragic in its emptiness, the little household duties for women, encouraged in an earlier and simpler age, had now gone out of date, while the modern idea of work in the great world was not so much as thought of. In a place like Brighton there were hundreds, perhaps, of households, in which girls were growing up with but one idea in life, that of taking their 'proper place in society'. A few meagre accomplishments − plentiful balls and dinner-parties, theatres and concerts − and to loaf up and down the parade, criticizing each other, were the means to bring about this desirable result! There was absolutely nothing else to do or live for.[5]

When they were all still young there were activities they could share. Carpenter used to go walking with his sister Ellen, who liked sketching, and talk of adventure in foreign lands. With Lizzie he played Beethoven, developing the love of music which was to stay with him all his life. But as he grew older his sisters' predicament made him depressed when he returned home. His six sisters had nothing to do

except dabble in paints and music . . . and wander aimlessly from room to room to see if by any chance 'anything was going on' . . . every aspiration and outlet except in the direction of dress and dancing was blocked; and marriage with the growing scarcity of men was becoming every day less likely or easy to compass. . . . Multiply this picture by thousands and hundreds of thousands all over the country, and it is easy to see how, when the causes of the misery were understood, it led to the powerful growth of the modern 'Women's Movement'.[6]

The other side of this helpless interior life was the man's complete and lonely absorption in the external things of the world. The financial cares of the family were the sole responsibility of his father. Politics belonged to the male's outside life. It did not occur to his father that his radical-liberal inclinations might affect the upbringing of his daughters. An emotional emptiness expanded as the years passed and direct feeling gave way to an habitual dependence on his wife. Sophia Carpenter died in 1881, worn out with the ceaseless effort of smoothing her husband's and children's domestic existence, only regretting that illness and old age made her no longer able to be useful to them. Ironically, after her death, his father 'woke from dreamland when it was too late', realising 'the mainspring is broken'.[7] He died a year later in April 1882.

A young upper-middle-class man had more freedom than a woman, but only within the confines of privilege. There were a few years at Oxford or Cambridge in which he could quest for his soul or sow wild oats. Edward Carpenter was a quester not a sower. His sexual awareness was constricted when he was young. When he had heard sex discussed by boys at school it left him unaffected if bewildered. His was a 'strangely slow-growing temperament';[8] he carried instead 'that other desire of the heart'. He turned to Tennyson, Wordsworth and Shelley. In the late 1860s he had been shown Rossetti's edition of Walt Whitman's poems and later obtained his own copies of *Leaves of Grass* and *Democratic Vistas*. Whitman's love of nature and commitment to freedom and comradeship attracted him but he still did not make the connection with his personal sense of dislocation. Whitman's influence remained intellectual; his own verses were conventional and cautious in form. It was not until later when he was twenty-five that he discovered 'with a great leap of joy . . . the treatment of sex which accorded with my own sentiments'.[9]

In 1868 he became a lecturer at Trinity Hall, Cambridge, and was elected to a clerical fellowship and ordained a deacon the following year. But he had not realised the extent to which the Broad Church openness of his background had taken him away from the assumptions of orthodox Anglicanism. Even when the sympathetic and heterodox F.D.Maurice became incumbent of St Edwards, Cambridge, Carpenter felt uneasy with his work as his curate. It was not only a question of doctrine. Observing that his ministry was completely alien and remote from the lives of the poor, he had an 'insuperable *feeling* of falsity and dislocation'.[10]

His sermon notes written in the early 1870s show him struggling with doubts stimulated by the Paris Commune, the programme of the First International and influenced by the ideas of the Italian nationalist Mazzini and by English radicalism. 'We . . . can only live on what is produced by the work of all the workers in England.'[11]

He wondered what the working class thought when they see, 'walking about the streets vast numbers of young men whose only idea appears to be dressed correctly and to think a good deal about themselves'.

He added, but then erased, 'numbers of young women whose life is spent on crochet work and evening parties'.[12]

He addressed his Cambridge congregation on the duties of the rich, the danger of a rising of the poor in anger against the parasitic leisure of the upper classes. He pressed his anxiety home with a Ruskinian warning of the consequences of irresponsible privilege. 'If we have hoodwinked this thing, this huge human creature and made it our beast of burden, what if it one day came to know this and shrug up its back and shake us into the dirt.'[13]

He still saw the working class as a threatening abstract force. Workers are still the 'creature' of middle-class imaginings. But he gives the 'creature' – 'this thing' – moral justification for insurrection. Fear plays on guilt and detaches him from the complacencies of his class.

By May 1871 the spiritual and intellectual crisis had become physical and he left his curacy to recuperate. On his return in October he took up his lecturing and college work but not his church duties. He sought within Christianity for a new social order and hoped that class feeling might be appeased but he could not continue to be a clergyman. The contradiction between his notion of Christ's gospel and everyday religious practice was too sharp. However, he was still unhappy in the confines of Cambridge academic life. This persistent personal unhappiness with his class and sex predicament was to take him towards more unconventional politics.

He went for a holiday to Italy in 1873 where he seemed to see Whitman's vision in Greek sculpture, man at one with nature. Italy was the symbolic alternative to late Victorian middle-class English values.

He also met a woman called Jane Olivia Daubeny, a connection by marriage to his family, who gave him the courage to live according to his own inclinations. When he met her she was in her fifties, still 'handsome' but an outcast from polite society because she had left her husband when he was unfaithful to her and had refused to collude in a sham. He wrote about the difficulties of Jane Olivia Daubeny's life without the protection of a husband under the pseudonym of 'Francesca' in *Sketches from Life*. Yet again he realised the narrow and stifling options open to women and the unnecessary suffering caused by sexual ignorance.

When a bright girl of some education and culture, and no doubt full of sentiments and ideals, marries what may be called the average man of her own class, she is not unlikely in the first few weeks or months, to go through a disillusioning process, of its kind one of the most trying of mortal experiences. Completely ignorant as she probably is, of certain sides of life, having little notion what marriage is, but only a rather vague sentiment in the place of knowledge, she finds herself at close quarters with a mate who suffers perhaps from the opposite defect – who knows somewhat too much, and too prosaically about the world. She comes with a shock against the rudest practicalities. And hardly less shocked is she to discover – as she thinks – an incurable brutality in the male mind. Her Sir Galahad turns into a commonplace boor with boorish sex-needs. Love itself seems to be simply dragged into the mire.[14]

Again past intensities are glanced over in *My Days and Dreams*. Carpenter describes Daubeny as an intellectual influence, only hinting at emotional connection. Her letters to him indicate much stronger feelings on her side – even passion for the unusual and sensitive young man who seemed to identify so much with her lonely resistance. She told him to leave Cambridge and helped him to choose his own life. He had also an immediate and personal reason for leaving Cambridge. He had made a close friendship at college with a young man from a relatively poor background called Andrew Beck who also loved poetry. Their friendship was not just a matter of intellectual sympathy, 'there was a touch of romance in our attachment'.[15] Evenings passed with their writing, they went on holidays together – until Beck changed and the poetry dried in him. Beck sought instead a respectable married life as an academic. The effect of this desertion is smoothed over in Carpenter's autobiography for Beck became Master of Trinity Hall and even a touch of romance could have compromised him. 'His mind', wrote Carpenter, 'took on a slightly cynical cast.'[16]

The letter in which Beck severed the relationship was more dramatic in its denial of the romance and poetry between them and indicates the strength of masculine bourgeois culture when it came to claim its own:

I looked at the rising moon unmoved. I wad my mental ears against all manner of sentiments – I will not allow myself to cry out or ache inwardly at any sorrow or any injustice. I systematically train myself into a consistent brutality. I'm utterly changed, it is all the reaction from you.[17]

In resisting the moon Beck could regain the privileges of his sex and class. His retreat from tenderness and cultivation of brutality was required of upper-class men. To be a man was to be a brute despite the civilised veneer of dress-coat and classical education. How else could the sons of the ruling class be bred for domination over workers, women and the empire. Just as the stereotype of female passivity developed when middle-class women ceased to play any part in production, a stereotype of masculinity hardened from the middle of the century. Though the more sensitive of the Victorians were conscious of their loss in denying tenderness and affection. 'I am past thirty and three parts iced over,'[18] Matthew Arnold told his friend, Clough, in 1853. The connection between withholding emotion, a kind of thrift of the senses, and manliness created an obsessive fear of love between men, which appears with particular intensity in the last quarter of the century. Sentiment, which had been acceptable in the mid-nineteenth century, was regarded in a new light. Tennyson's *In Memoriam* was even suspect, though the loved one was dead. Self-consciousness flickers throughout the poem. There are hints of 'inner vileness' and 'hidden shame' even in the most spiritual of loves.[19] Coming to consciousness at a time when even Tennyson was seen as effeminate reading, Carpenter was to be a crucial figure in the anti-Victorian rebellion which asserted not only tenderness among men but the freedom of the body and of the senses. Already in the 1870s he sought an alternative notion of manliness in which love was possible and in which 'manly attachment' would not be betrayed. He identified with Walt Whitman's exaltation of the male body in *Calamus*.

> I proceed for all who are or have been young men
> To tell the secret of my nights and days,
> To celebrate the need of comrades.[20]

Whitman was not ashamed of physical longings and sought the outcast and outlawed. In *I am he that aches with love* he wrote:

> The echoes ring with our indecent calls,
>     I pick out some low person for my dearest friend,
> He shall be lawless, rude illiterate, he shall be
>     one condemned by others for deeds done,
> I will play a part no longer, why should I
>     exile myself from my companions.[21]

In July 1874 Carpenter wrote a remarkable letter to Walt Whitman in America about the significance of the poet's writings for himself and for others, in which he expressed contempt for the commercialism and respectability of Victorian society and searched for change.

And here though dimly, I think I see the new, open life which is to come. The spirit moving backwards and forwards beneath the old forms, strengthening and reshaping the foundation before it alters the superstructure.

Carpenter saw two sources for this new life, 'women' and 'artisans'. He does not explain how he saw the women's role but it is likely he had encountered women in radical academic circles at Cambridge like Millicent Fawcett, Anne Jemima Clough and Emily Davies who were involved in agitation for the vote, for education, work, and the right of women to own their own property. He may also have known of Josephine Butler's campaign against the Contagious Diseases Acts, which had divided the feminist groupings because it touched on sexuality and implied a woman's right over her own body. His feelings about the 'artisans' are more immediate. He told Whitman about a young workman who came to mend his door, 'with the old divine light in his eyes'. He thanked Walt Whitman for giving him:

a ground for the love of men . . . For you have made men to be not ashamed of the noblest instinct of their nature. Women are beautiful but to some, there is that which passes the love of women.

Carpenter felt his personal liberation to be bound up with a wider social awakening.

Between the splendid dawn of Greek civilisation and the high universal noon of Democracy there is a strange horror of darkness on us (but) slowly I think the fetters are falling from men's feet, the cramps and crazes of the old superstitions are relaxing, the idiotic ignorance of class contempt is dissipating.

Self-realisation was inseparable from new forms of relationship and democratic comradeship.

If men shall learn to accept one another simply and without complaint – if they shall . . . honour the free immeasurable gift of their own personality, delight in it and bask in it without false shames and affectations.

He told Whitman far away in Canada, 'Now I am going away to lecture to the working men and women in the North. They at least desire to lay hold of something with a real grasp.'[22]

He was referring to his plans for teaching in the University Extension Movement. This was an organisation started by James Stuart, a young Cambridge radical, in response to pressure from Northern co-operators and women in Cambridge and the North of England who were trying to develop women's higher education. Stuart hoped that his peripatetic teachers would educate all classes together and that a common culture would heal class resentment. The classes were to pay for the lecturers' fees but the university, first Cambridge, followed by Oxford and other universities provided a central office or delegacy. Many of Carpenter's contemporaries went to work in University Extension wanting especially to teach the newly enfranchised working-class electorate. Many of them were anxious to disprove economic ideas of land nationalisation, concerned to connect workers to traditions of liberal constitutional government or to uplift the philistines with sweetness and light. With Carpenter it was a little different. He was less confident as a representative of his class and as a missionary of culture. He was too unhappy with his own social predicament and with upper-middle-class values to fit in to the dominant ethos of the University Extension Movement. He already wanted to learn from workers as much as to teach. He wanted to find himself in an ideal of the common life and sought an alternative to the detachment and insincerity of academic and fashionable circles.

E.M.Forster said of his move, 'With him it was really a case of social maladjustment. He wasn't happy in the class in which he was born. . . . He didn't revolt from a sense of duty, or to make a splash, but because he wanted to.'[23]

## University Extension and Radicalism in Sheffield

The North was not quite what he imagined. He found soot and provincial respectability, suffered indigestion from landladies' cooking and was hurtled about in what seemed like unending railways on his lecturing circuit. As he scrambled around on astronomy outings, peering at the murky stars through polluted industrial skies with his young lady students, he must have cast wry thoughts over the Atlantic to Walt Whitman. Although sympathetic to the movement for women's education, he kept his distance from most of the women who organised Extension classes through the Leeds Ladies' Educational Association. However, he made a lasting friendship with the Ford sisters who lived at Adel Grange and like him were drawn towards socialism in the next few years. He also renewed his friendship with Charles Oates who lived at Meanwood and whom he had known at college. By 1877 he was able to break away from an exclusively middle-class milieu and could tell Oates, 'There are some nice people in Sheffield but most of those I know are of the non-respectable class.'[24]

He also began to write about the poverty he saw around him

in Sheffield and about his own feelings of class estrangement. The notes from this period formed the basis of his Whitmanic poem *Towards Democracy*. More publicly in his lectures he was already beginning to touch on problems which were to preoccupy him later. He struggled against the acceptance of a vulgar materialism. Sceptical about religion he was still reluctant to abandon the quest for an inner consciousness which could transcend matter. A longing for simplicity and directness in human relationships was already evident.[25] He was to find something of this openness when he met Walt Whitman in America in 1877. American culture as a whole seemed to have a welcome 'rough freedom', and 'ease' and 'independence' which still eluded him in Britain. He caught a tantalising glimpse of his Whitmanic ideal of democratic comrade-ship in the body of a young man, Joe Potter, whom he used to watch run in the ancient foot-races in Sheffield, where the participants were only clad in a thin strip between the legs. But Potter went to sea and they lost contact. He was searching for open friendship as much as physical beauty.

His encounter with two of his students, a scythe-maker, Albert Fearnehough, and his friend, Charles Fox, was of more lasting significance. Fearnehough was stolid and meticulous, preoccupied with his craft. Fox was a small farmer and self-taught philosopher, sceptical of religion, sharp and observant under a surface of country slowness. He was deeply resistant to the commercial world which surrounded him and attached to quiet physical pleasures. He liked his tobacco and drank perhaps more than was good for him. He was concerned about the seasons, wry about thrift, contemptuous of sanctimony and of polite society. Carpenter's sketch of him as *Martin Turner* is among his warmest and most affectionate writings. He must have symbolised for Carpenter the new roots which he sought. He gradually met men and women active in the radical movement. Through them he encountered an alternative which carried still something of the communitarian vision of early nineteenth-century socialism. There was Joseph Sharpe, a wandering harpist and free thinker who used to tramp the country lanes, communing with the stars and playing at

local fairs. Sharpe had been a Chartist and drilled in the quarries
of Mount Sorrell, Leicestershire. He lived to carry socialist and
anarchist propaganda into the smaller villages. There was
Jonathan Taylor too who had come to Sheffield in 1863 and was
from a Chartist family. He would speak at the old pump at West
Bar on radical subjects and campaigned for free education. There
were links with the Owenites as well as with Chartism. The
Sheffield secularists met in the 1870s in the Owenite Hall of Science
and in their celebrations and outings resembled the utopian
socialists in their emphasis on an alternative culture. The
communitarian tradition had never really died in the Sheffield area
perhaps because a structure of small workshop production and
small holdings persisted. In the mid 1870s a group of secularists,
Quakers and Unitarians who met in a mutual improvement group,
decided to live communally. Their plan to buy land and farm it was
speeded up by John Ruskin who provided money through the St
George's Guild. But Ruskin saw the Guild as a paternalistic return
to harmonious master–servant relations which would solve the
class conflict brought by competition and the cash-nexus. The
communitarians did not want a master and trouble soon broke out
between them and Ruskin. St George's farm at Totley ended in
bitterness and recriminations which were still strong a decade later
when the old controversy was brought up in *Commonweal* and one
of the settlers, M.A.Maloy, put their case.

A socialist called John Harrison Riley who had
propagandised in London and Bristol before coming to Sheffield
was employed by Ruskin to look after the venture. He found
himself in the uncomfortable position of being attacked from both
sides. Totley broke Riley's faith in creating the new moral world in
England. He emigrated to Massachusetts in 1880. But while he was
still at Totley he met Edward Carpenter and visited Fox and
Fearnehough in nearby Bradway, bringing socialist propaganda.
Riley had learned his socialism from the followers of the Chartist
Bronterre O'Brien in the First International who thought the
solution to social problems was the nationalisation and co-
operative colonisation of the land.

Carpenter, dissatisfied with lodging in the city, moved first to Bradway and then to Totley in May 1880. He tried to intercede unsuccessfully on Riley's behalf with Ruskin and eventually provided new tenants for St George's Farm who were also communitarians. Among the new group was a mystical Christian socialist who had started life as a Methodist lay preacher, John Furniss. Furniss was a quarryman and, like Jonathan Taylor, a popular outdoor speaker. He would stride into Sheffield with his friend, George Pearson, who leased the farm five or six miles over the moors, to speak at the Pump or the Monolith.

In the 1870s dreams of the new moral world did not completely die because there was no means of putting them into effect. This period remains relatively unstudied but the emergent socialism of the 1880s is incomprehensible without an understanding of the earlier radical context. In Sheffield, radicals oscillated between trying to put their ideas into practice in small utopian experiments or supporting particular radical campaigns. Sheffield had a proud history of municipal radicalism going back to the Chartist, Isaac Ironside, through to Plimsoll, Mundella and J.Wilson. A network of radical clubs began to form a base for working-class radicalism in the Liberal Party. By the early 1880s a distinct grouping had emerged and, impatient with pressurising the Liberal establishment, were preparing to put up their own candidate, Mervyn Hawkes. Hawkes' campaign in 1885 had the support of a radical local paper, the *Sheffield Weekly Echo*, subtitled first 'An anti-Whig Journal' and later 'The Yorkshire Free Press'. He stood for the reform of Parliament, Irish Home Rule, free education, 'root and branch' land reform, religious equality, temperance reform and a strong navy. Jonathan Taylor and John Furniss were among his supporters who also included Carpenter.[26] These supporters appear to have been more radical than their own candidate.

John Furniss' speech at a meeting in November 1885 expresses an extreme radicalism with a strong sense of the workers' distinct and separate interests:

Is ours a people's Parliament? We are told the Liberals are friends of the people. I don't want friends of the people, I want the people (cheers). Working men manage to create wealth and can therefore manage Parliamentary affairs (Hear, hear, and applause). I hope the necessary educated class will be our own. I do not want to entrust my interests to the hands of a party whose whole education has been to rob me. I have no confidence in any capitalists. The whole association of their lives runs counter to the workers' interests. I don't want 'liberal parties'. I want justice not liberality. I want to manage my own affairs. If the workers only get the same idea neither party will be able to dislodge it. My party is the people. When the day of humanity shall dawn we shall know how to deal with them . . . [the landed aristocracy, the moneyocracy].[27]

The Liberal establishment survived Hawkes' candidature but the radicals involved in the campaign emerged convinced with Furniss that the workers should manage their own affairs, that the land should be held in common, that labour created wealth and that the Liberal Party could not express their class interests. Several of the men and women involved were to form the nucleus of the socialist club a year later. The impact of this working-class radicalism combining with the utopian communitarian tradition must have strengthened Carpenter's lonely search for an alternative to capitalism and confirmed his theoretical interest in Mazzini, the First International and the Commune. The mystical search for a closeness to nature of a man like Joseph Sharpe fed Carpenter's own inner longing for communion without a Christian God.

His mother's death in 1880 followed by his father's soon after had left him economically independent and free to give up Extension lecturing and settle in the country. His reading of the *Bhagavad-Gita* and his writing of *Towards Democracy* from April 1881 helped him to realise inner spiritual changes. His move into the country created a break with his earlier pattern of life,

it seemed to liberate the pent-up emotionality of years. All the feelings which had sought, in suffering and in distress, their stifled expression within me during the last seven or eight years, gathered themselves together to a new and more joyous utterance.

He felt physically renewed, his senses were open to sounds, 'there was a new beauty over the world'. He became conscious of 'some intimation of a perpetual freedom and gladness such as the earth and its inhabitants . . . had hardly yet dreamed of'. An image haunted him, 'a vision within me of something like the bulb and bud, with short green blades of a huge hyacinth just appearing above the ground', the image was one of 'vigour and abounding life'. Later he felt that it was a sign 'that my life had really at last taken root and was beginning rapidly to grow'.[28]

In 1883 he took a small-holding at Millthorpe and Albert Fearnehough and his wife came to help him. He found it hard work and worried because he could not achieve the solitude and serenity of Thoreau's *Walden*. The American transcendentalists were a continuing influence though he was to reject a purely individual search for inner harmony. When he went to America to see Whitman again in 1884, he threw a stone into Walden Pond, paying his tribute to Thoreau. While in America he also visited the Rileys on their farm in Massachusetts.

Between 1883 and 1885 his ideas were tending towards socialism 'with a drift . . .'towards Anarchism'. His socialism was closely connected to his vision of growth, new life and roots. A lecture he gave in the Hall of Science on Co-operative Production and the French thinker, Leclaire, in 1883 gives an idea of his politics. He expressed a moral indignation against the effects of competition based on the conditions he had seen in the Sheffield workshops. The sources for his radicalism are Leclaire's theories of co-operative production and Ruskin's views on the dignity of labour. This ethical concern forced him to ask why there could be poverty amidst plenty while the land remained unused and unproductive. This concern must have been influenced by the communal farming he had encountered in Sheffield and by ideas of land nationalisation among radicals. His politics were still formed by the emphasis on the land and by Mazzini and Ruskin's stress on the duty of the rich. There is also the idea of possessing your own culture strong in popular radicalism; in the future co-operative society ordinary people would become heroes and heroines of history. He hoped that the 'simplest life' would be recognised 'as good as any'. His exaltation of communality went beyond the poor to the outcast. Like the romantics and like Whitman he saw the degraded as carrying the new world. We could identify 'our common humanity' in the despised, in 'the troubled and wandering eyes of the crazy and insane'.[29] This early faith in a hidden human nature, locked against itself by oppressive social relationships, escaping from restraint only among the most wretched of victims, was to play a crucial part both in his socialism and in his writing about sexual liberation.

### The New Life

In the early 1880s socialism was beginning to have some impact upon popular radicalism, though the old moral enthusiasm and the emphasis upon creating an alternative culture persisted in the working-class movement. Its influence was felt not only by workers. Some middle-class intellectuals and artists were drawn towards groups like the Progressive Association, the Fellowship of the New Life, the Fabians and the Social Democratic Federation. Carpenter read H.M.Hyndman's popularising work *England for All* in 1883, and made his way to a meeting of the SDF in Westminster Bridge Road, London. Through the SDF he met William Morris, two ex-Eton schoolmasters, Jim Joynes and Henry Salt — who had moved towards socialism via the land nationaliser Henry George, Shelley and vegetarianism — and Kate Joynes who married Henry Salt. The Salts were to remain close friends for many years, living for some time in a cottage near Millthorpe.[30] He was also to meet Havelock Ellis and Olive Schreiner through the Fellowship of the New Life.

As yet there was still no clear division between marxists who sought to change the external forms of social relationships in the SDF and those who were more preoccupied with inner spiritual transformation like Havelock Ellis. Radical ideas about simplifying life and living without servants in order not to be parasites on others combined with the elevation of manual work which came from Ruskin. The politics of land nationalisation merged with a populist conception of country people as both wise and innocent. There were schemes for communities in which household work was divided equally between classes and between the sexes. The emphasis of all these ideas was upon forming new personal relationships. They were not abstract notions about society but a new way of living. The questioning of conventional sexual morality and of the position of women came as part of this social movement among the intelligentsia. It was to have an influence not only upon the middle class but upon some working-class socialists.

Although they were in rebellion against Victorian bourgeois orthodoxy they retained many of their parents' values. If they rejected Christianity they continued to struggle within a religious idiom. Earnest endeavour and the inner voice were central to their structure of feeling.

Havelock Ellis' friend, Olive Schreiner, a young South African feminist writer, is a good example of the struggle to combine openness in personal living with writing and political activity. It was an effort which exhausted her. She wrote to Carpenter from Whitby in May 1887:

It is only in work that has no connection with the self, that we can find rest to our spirits. Life, personal life, is a great battlefield. Those who enter it must fight. Those who enter it and will not fight get riddled with bullets. The only thing for them is to keep out of it and have no personal life. . . . One will never find a man to love, that some other woman does not desire.[31]

It was particularly difficult for the women within this radical milieu because the strain was doubly felt. Not only were they trying to live in a new way which challenged personal relationships within capitalist society, but they had also to resist their particular constraints as women in the late nineteenth century.

Olive Schreiner watched her friends Kate Salt and Eleanor Marx struggle and be crushed. She survived – but only with the pain she recorded in her writings, *Story of an African Farm*, *From Man to Man*, or *Stories, Dreams and Allegories*. Schreiner was one of the founders of the Social Democratic Federation Women's League as well as a member of the Fellowship of the New Life, with Ellis. She worked in the South African radical movement later and supported the suffrage movement but her feeling for change could never be contained within political movements which related only to the outer fabric.

Among this radical intelligentsia there was a strong impulse towards the land and manual work. Carpenter was not alone in living in a cottage in the country. There was quite a return to the land in the early 1880s among his acquaintances although they tended to be part-time cottagers. Olive Schreiner, the Salts, Eleanor Marx, Ellis, and Edith Lees whom he married later, all spent time in rural retreats. It was partly for convenience and partly a search for the 'people'. Harold Cox, a university friend of Carpenter's, took a cottage at Farnham, Surrey. Just opposite, Henry Salt was busy writing articles for the SDF paper *Justice* which Carpenter had helped to start with money from the income his father left him. Goldsworthy Lowes Dickinson went down there to prepare University Extension lectures in April 1885.[32] Following Edward Carpenter into adult teaching he was even less happy than Carpenter had been. In the early 1880s he was searching along with his friend, Charles Ashbee, for some reconciliation between the spirit and social action. The influence of Ruskin was very evident. The feeling that mental work was unbalanced and worthless, that they were parasites living off the producers who were the workers was a theme in Lowes Dickinson and Ashbee's correspondence in the early 1880s. But they were not able to reconcile self-fulfilment, identification with the workers, manual work and socialism as harmoniously as Carpenter. Lowes Dickinson wrote to Ashbee in January 1885 'for me not to reform the working man but myself is now the problem for is not the working man one who can make? and I one who can make nought.'[33]

Lowes Dickinson went to Farnham with an idyllic notion of an unspoilt peasantry. Not surprisingly he was disappointed to find, instead of his communal egalitarians, conservative voters irritated by the Liberal tax on beer. As for the dignity of manual labour he was a complete failure, writing in dismay to Ashbee in May 1885, 'I cannot milk a cow'.[34]

Ashbee was more socially radical than Lowes Dickinson. He felt he could not become an architect when land was privately owned. He rejected the philanthropic complacency of Toynbee Hall and sought a more democratic fellowship through the creation of a Guild and School of Handicraft. Through the Guild he hoped for comradeship, interpreted as the gospel of work – 'something real as against the theoretic talk ... human intimacies and a community of free men'.[35] Carpenter's Whitmanite vision of male comrades and socialism as a new religion were attractive to him. But he was as shocked by London radical workers who seemed disrespectful and materialistic as Lowes Dickinson was by the country people of Surrey. He began to see the Guild as an alternative to socialism, which earned him William Morris' hearty contempt.

Both Lowes Dickinson and Ashbee went into political retreat in the following decade but in the '80s there was still a state of flux within which opinions could change as well as polarise. There were always arguments. Roger Fry, a Cambridge friend who shared their aesthetic concerns, was doubtful from the start about Ashbee and Lowes Dickinson's attempts at social commitment. Hyndman and the Webbs argued with the Salts in their cottage in Farnham. Shaw dithered between irony and sympathy for personal politics, while Hyndman told him off:

I do not want the movement to be a depository of old cranks, humanitarians, vegetarians, anti-vivisectionists and anti-vaccinationists, arty-crafties and all the rest of them, we are scientific socialists and have no room for sentimentalists. They confuse the issue.[36]

When, towards the end of 1884, William Morris and other members of the SDF, broke with Hyndman and formed the Socialist League, Carpenter and his circle inclined towards them. They gave less importance to building an organisation and waiting for the crisis and much more to the creation of a new consciousness and culture. They were critical of the SDF's acceptance of immediate reforms for they believed revolution was imminent and were concerned about the quality of life in the new society. *Commonweal* – the paper of the Socialist League – announced 'Edward Carpenter' on 'Private Property' at the Farringdon Hall in January 1886.[37] They wanted personal transformation as much as change in ownership but even in the early days wondered sometimes if this were possible. Lowes Dickinson and Ashbee heard Carpenter speak on the same subject to the Hammersmith Socialist League with William Morris in the chair. Charles Ashbee remembered how 'Goldie' drew Morris out later on the principles of socialism and how he warmed to his subject, banging his fist on the table and saying, 'The thing is this: if we had our Revolution tomorrow what should we Socialists do the day after. "Yes! what?" we all cried. And that he could not answer. "We should all be hanged, because we are promising the people more than we can ever give them."'

Undaunted by this gloomy future Ashbee and 'Goldie' left in excitement with Edward Carpenter and the 'Miss Carpenters'. After the Carpenters departed they walked home with Bernard Shaw 'the socialist' from Hammersmith discussing 'the coming Revolution' and the collapse of the capitalist system. Though 'Goldie' said after Shaw left them at Tottenham Court Road that he did not feel 'any forrader with Socialism'.[38]

A year later he had plunged back into introspection and doubt about his commitment.

The natural attitude is to stand apart and learn. But that again ain't allowed. Because the unemployed shriek to one 'Are you not a man and a brother?' and all one's soul cries out yes and has to leave its philosophic contemplation to do so.[39]

He was not to reconcile the two but remained interested in how Carpenter effected the combination he found so difficult. In Lowes Dickinson's memoir of Carpenter, he described asking how he did it to which Carpenter breezily replied that 'he liked to hang out his red flag from the ground floor and then go up above to see how it looked'.[40]

Carpenter's politics were important in maintaining the connections of the early '80s during the next two decades. He was to show a peculiar resilience in struggling against the inner and outer bondages though their relationship was not quite as easy as he implied to Lowes Dickinson. This resilience was not simply a matter of his own temperament. It is likely that an isolated quest for ideal community would have exhausted itself and that Edward Carpenter would have been compelled to make peace, like many other middle-class rebels of the early '80s, with the values of his class. Instead his politics were to be sustained because they were located within the radical and communitarian traditions of South Yorkshire and Derbyshire.

### The Sheffield Socialists

For Carpenter socialism and the inner life were not alternatives. His involvements and friendships with men like Furniss and Sharpe and his links with Sheffield radicalism in the 1870s and very early '80s meant that his politics grew around his life in ways that they did not for his London and Cambridge friends. The formation of the socialist group in Sheffield confirmed the already existing radical nucleus. Once the group was started it meant meetings, propaganda excursions, socials, and eventually a socialist café. So he was inevitably immersed in local organising for several years. This day-to-day practical activity absorbed much time and emotion. It also meant a continuing relationship to a group of men and women who formed the core of the socialist club until a split occurred in the early '90s between anarchists and socialists.

In March 1886 Carpenter arranged for William Morris to speak. This meeting brought together the informal radical nucleus which had grown around Hawkes' candidature and a socialist society was formed. Morris was followed by a veteran of 1870s radicalism, John Sketchley. Carpenter took his young friend from Cambridge, Charles Ashbee, to hear Sketchley but Ashbee was scared by the speaker's radical insurrectionism and unconvinced by Sketchley's passion for statistics. He preferred Carpenter's socialism with its spirituality and love of comrades. Annie Besant, already a well-known speaker, came in April 1886 to the socialist club. Carpenter had met her in London left circles and they remained in contact with one another.[41]

The Sheffield socialists could also draw on local speakers. There was Raymond Unwin from Chesterfield, then working as an engineer for the Staveley Coal and Iron Company. Unwin had been affected by similar influences to Carpenter. He had worked at Charles Rowley's settlement at Ancoats in Manchester. Influenced by Whitman and Morris, he was interested in planning new communities. This interest was stimulated by Morris' ideas and his knowledge of St George's Farm at Totley and Carpenter's house at Millthorpe. As the years went by this utopian communitarian connection became looser and planning came to predominate for Unwin. He designed the first garden city, Letchworth. But the subject of the talk he gave in the summer of 1886 indicates how important communitarianism on the land still was for socialists. Communism still meant communal living, not marxism. In *Communism in the Past and what it teaches* Unwin ranged through the village communities in Europe, Peru, China, Mexico, with special emphasis on the Russian unit and the Serbian family.[42]

Carpenter himself spoke early in July; he was described by a reporter from the local radical paper, *The Sheffield Weekly Echo*, as 'tall, spare, with browned bearded face'. He spoke 'plainly' of his personal experience on the land, arguing for nationalisation and communal farms. 'We should not then work for profit, but because things require to be done.' They assembled in the upper room of the Wentworth Café, Holly Street, an old radical haunt. Before the meeting began there were:

A dozen people, mostly working-men . . . waiting on bare forms or on chairs. . . . In front stood a table covered with papers and pamphlets of a Socialist character for sale or distribution. There was no rush for seats; one by one the numbers increased, but still the choicely respectable element was conspicuous by its absence.

The elder part of the Socialistic audiences, which included several women, were evidently of the hard-working sort into whose lives not too much joy of existence had entered. They were there to hear if under some more rational and just arrangement of society they and theirs could not work and live without losing all that life is worth in a hopeless interminable struggle to exist.[43]

Forty-four people signed the Sheffield Socialists' Manifesto in 1886; it was overwhelmingly male; forty-one men, three women. The manifesto declared:

The present state of Society being founded on the landlord and the capitalist system, by which one man is enabled to live on the labour of another, society being consequently divided, roughly speaking into two classes – poor workers and rich idlers. It is therefore the object of this association to aid in the abolition of this system – and so to bring about a regenerate society in which everyone who can shall work – those incapable of working being provided for by the community.[44]

The socialists aimed to end the 'monopolies' of land and capital by land nationalisation and the gradual nationalisation of the large industries. They supported a cumulative income tax, labour representation in parliament, councils, boards of guardians and school boards. They were ready to co-operate with other societies which supported these ideas.[45]

The members of the society were a mixed bunch politically. They included ex-Chartists, secularists, members of both groups of Totley communitarians, Christian Socialists and radicals. In *My Days and Dreams*, Carpenter said they were to reach numbers of a hundred or more, with a dozen or twenty forming 'the moving and active element'.[46] Among these he mentions the Bingham brothers and their sister, Louisa Usher.[47] Although not especially close to him personally, they were important figures in the society. All three were active, Usher in the campaign for Hawkes, along with Furniss, Taylor, Drury, Peach, Storey, Garbutt and Carpenter.[48] Apart from Louisa Usher, Mrs Maloy seems to have been the only other woman who played a prominent role in the group. It is not clear whether she was the 'M.A.Maloy' who appears writing to *Commonweal* about St George's Farm at Totley[49] – though it was unusual for women to be known in socialist circles by initials rather than a full name.

Carpenter's close personal friends among the socialists were George and Fannie Hukin, George and Lucy Adams, Jim Shortland and James Brown when he moved to the Sheffield area from Glasgow, and Raymond Unwin who often visited. He said he found 'fraternity and fellowship' with the Sheffield socialists. They were working for a 'dream and an ideal, that of the common life conjoined to the free individuality . . . they hailed William Morris and his work with the most sincere appreciation.'[50] Writing to a friend in the mid-1880s, he contrasted his socialist friends with the radical workers:

We have some very good fellows among our Socialist Society. I must say *that* type is far preferable to the so-called Radicals. As a rule I hate *them* – cantankerous argumentative animals – but the socts [sic] are generally as far as I have seen them, warmhearted and of a sympathetic cast.[51]

George Hukin was one of these early close comrades. He was of Dutch descent and had a razor-grinding business with his brother. He lived in Bath Street, Sheffield, and later in a cottage near Carpenter at Holmesfield with Fannie whom he married in 1888. Carpenter describes him at work *In the Stone-floored Workshop*, emerging after work 'a figure with dusty cap and light curls escaping from under it, large dark grey eyes and Dutch-featured face of tears and laughter'.[52] There was a very private George Hukin, who was a keen gardener and loved walking. But he was also deeply political in a quiet way. He was not a public speaker 'but though young an excellent help at our committee meetings'.[53] Carpenter relied on his and George Adams' accounts of the Socialist Society. Hukin, in particular, gives the unofficial picture of the day-to-day doings of the club. He was for Carpenter 'First and most trusted of my Sheffield socialist "comrades"'[54] and 'always from the beginning a special ally of mine.'

George Hukin was also a close friend of George Adams who Carpenter says was 'town bred, rather slight and thin with a forward stoop and a shock of black hair', and had 'an impetuous, humorous and rather artistic temperament – not too exact or precise about details, but one who could cover a good deal of ground in a day'.[55] His father, a cobbler, who drank, died when he was thirteen. Poverty had made him resourceful and George Adams went to an orphange which had recently opened in the poor area of Sheffield in which he lived. They tried to turn him away because it was only for girls but he refused to go and so they made a boys' side to the orphange. After about a year he went to work cleaning knives and boots for a Sheffield manufacturer and later became an under-gardener. He loved drawing and painting and his employers let him go for lessons in an art school. When he was twenty he left and earned his living as an insurance-collector, but he really liked gardening and painting. When the Fearnehoughs departed he and his wife, Lucy, left 279 Queen Street and went to work on Carpenter's small-holding, where George gardened and learned sandal-making. Harold Armitage, a reporter on the *Sheffield Independent*, remembered Lucy Adams, in the mid-'80s as 'a blue-eyed golden-haired girl with pink and white complexion'.[56] She was also involved in the Socialist Society. Carpenter and Adams fell out in the 1890s which is why Carpenter says Adams was 'a good friend and a good hater'.[57] But in the early years of the society he was close to him. Both the Hukins and the Adams were young in the mid '80s and do not appear to have been involved in previous political work.

In the summer of 1886 the socialists started holding open-air meetings at the corner of Fargate and Surrey Street, continuing a well-established radical tradition. On 28 August, S.W.Drury of Attercliffe, John Rivelin and Edward Carpenter spoke on socialism to between two hundred and three hundred people. Drury, apparently a Christian Socialist, said they wanted a society based 'on the teaching of Christ "Thou shalt love thy neighbour as thyself"', in opposition to the false society of today, whose motto is "Each for himself and the devil take the hindmost"'. Rivelin explained that the rich were not the brethren of the poor but 'preying on their vitals'. Carpenter attacked rent and interest, especially the money made by railway shareholders, which he presumably knew about because of his father's investments.

R.F.Muirhead of the Glasgow Branch of the Socialist League, then gave an account of the movement in Glasgow. This early link with Glasgow and Carpenter's friendship with the young mathematics teacher, Bob Muirhead, was to survive the collapse of the League and the accompanying factional bitterness. After the speeches 'an animated discussion followed in which Mrs Maloy took part; but the opposition was feeble, and the sense of the audience was strongly in favour of the Socialists.'[58]

Both the forms of these meetings and the moral sentiments of the speakers would have been familiar to people who had taken part in earlier radical activity. The religious and ethical preoccupations of the socialists in Sheffield also paralleled Carpenter's own religious struggle and his reluctance to accept a materialist explanation of society.

Their outdoor meetings provoked police interference in the summer of 1886. This brought some support from radicals like Jonathan Taylor, always ready to defend free speech causes.[59] There were social events in the radical café, small private meetings in people's houses to train speakers, outings and rambles – all similar to the activities of radicals and secularists in which the social life of the club was important. Like them the socialists thought naturally of the need for a social and political centre and searched in the winter of 1886–7 for a suitable place. In the spring they found a place in Scotland Street. The building, which had been an old debtors' jail, was called the 'Commonwealth Café'.[60] The club, which held 150 people, had a grand opening with Mahon back again and Tom Maguire, a young socialist from Leeds. Carpenter was in the chair and John Furniss and Rev Charles Peach, a Unitarian minister from Sheffield, spoke. Furniss talked about the Commonwealth, 'the common well-being of the common people. By common people he did not mean one class. He held that they were all common. They were of one common flesh and blood and their necessities were common.' He attacked the values of self-help and getting on. For every one man who succeeded, a thousand suffered:

They were told in their infancy, they heard it from pulpits that it was their duty to follow his example. But he had learned from a grand old book that there was another idea of man, that there was something that ministers didn't preach about at all. That book told him if he wanted to be happy, he must not do it by making others miserable.

He shared Ruskin's view of the meaning of the word 'property' – that which was proper to anyone. When Charles Peach spoke he paid tribute to Furniss' community and said that was what they were trying to work here – a little communism. He also denied that socialism was merely the expression of the interests of a class – it was the natural outcome of human nature craving for a freer and truer existence. Socialism was humanity working out its real divinity and he quoted Emerson in his support. Carpenter, who accompanied the songs which interspersed the speeches on a harmonium, spoke with a similar approach. Socialism 'was not merely a movement for the industrial emancipation of men; it meant the entire regeneration of society in art, in science, in religion and in literature; and the building up of a new life in which industrial socialism was the foundation'.[61]

They were eclectic still in their choice of speakers in 1887; the anarchists Kropotkin and Charlotte Wilson came, as well as Tom Maguire from the Socialist League and Mahon, who thought the League should be more involved in the struggle for the 8-hour day.[62]

Nonetheless the Sheffield society did not escape the political tensions which were being felt at the centre of the Socialist League. They had the same uncertainty about the relationship of immediate reforms to the long-term objective of communism. There was no clear recognition of the need to take part in day-to-day agitation in unions. This was evaded temporarily by participation in the much more dramatic unemployed demonstrations. The SDF had been working with the unemployed in London throughout 1887, but the Socialist League had kept aloof because they thought it was unprincipled to hold out hopes of a solution in capitalism. However, on 17, 18 and 19 October Trafalgar Square was cleared by mounted police using their batons. All meetings in Trafalgar Square were banned early in November. On 13 November in defiance of that ban the radicals and the Irish called a demonstration against the government's policy of coercion in Ireland and the Socialist League were swept into the campaign to keep the right to protest in the Square. Trafalgar Square was surrounded by police and armed soldiers. Morris and Annie Besant were with the Clerkenwell contingent and addressed them from a cart before the police attacked.[63] Edward Carpenter was there and was hit by a policeman. Both Hukin and Adams were upset he had not been able to retaliate. Hukin was enraged when he read the newspaper reports and thought it 'awfully galling not to be able to get at the peeler who struck you'.[64] Adams was sorry Carpenter had not been able 'to give a Roland for an Oliver' and thought it 'damn hard lines when they hit and run away'. The immediate response to 'Bloody Sunday' was a hardening of resolve. Adams wrote to Carpenter, 'The victory they steal today does not prove they will win tomorrow, and if it should not come while we live we can get some pleasure in dying fighting for it.'[65] George Hukin felt it 'ought to strengthen Morris' party'.[66] Both were disgusted with the 'Libs and Rads' because they had left the Square and gone to Hyde Park and Adams was dismayed that the radicals were to organise the demonstration the following Sunday. 'I suppose Bradlaugh has something to do with it; he wants some credit but doesn't want to fight them.'[67]

The next Sunday mounted police galloped up and down the Square. There were a large number of arrests and a bystander, Alfred Linnell, was knocked down by a horse, injured and died later. Radicals and socialists united for a massive demonstration in his memory.

The attack by the authorities on the left was an attempt to quell resistance to the government's repressive policy in Ireland and to break the small revolutionary socialist groups in England. The ruling class had been caught off-guard by unemployed riots in 1886 and were perhaps rattled as their own sons and daughters disappeared for a brief stay at Toynbee Hall, slumming. Morris described their two methods of dealing with resistance as force and fraud. When the latter failed they resorted to the former. 'Bloody Sunday' left many socialists in Britain more bitter, but it also put paid to any vaguely romantic ideas of an unresisted insurrection.

Repression was not limited to Britain. Bismarck passed his anti-socialist laws, forcing German socialists underground, and in America, that ironic land of the free, five anarchists in Chicago were accused of throwing a bomb in a demonstration in the Haymarket. One killed himself and four were executed on 12 November – the day before Bloody Sunday. The case had a tremendous impact on socialists in Britain and the trial and execution was reported in great detail by the radical press. The anarchist August Spies' words as he was being executed, 'there will come a time when our silence will be more powerful than the voices they are strangling to death now',[68] touched revolutionaries in Britain and seemed to express their own frustration and desperation.

Unemployment was severe in Sheffield by the end of 1887 and the Poor Law was quite unable to deal with the distress. The SDF had written early in November suggesting a united unemployed demonstration. George Hukin absentmindedly forgot to mention the letter, then talked to Storey and a few other socialists about it who thought 'it would be a capital thing' and that 'the Radical Club people would join us and help to make it a success'. They appointed a deputation to go and talk to the radicals and Hukin wrote to Drury in Attercliffe 'to see if he could get any of the unemployed together in his neighbourhood. I should think there must be a good many about in Attercliffe.'[69]

In mid-November George Adams went to tea in Bath Street with George and Fannie Hukin and Louisa Usher and then went round to the café to a meeting about the unemployed demonstration at which Jonathan Taylor and Thomas Garbutt from Attercliffe spoke. The radicals were refusing to have anything to do with it. 'I don't know what we shall make of it, it depends what the unemployed will do.'[70] Towards the end of November they held a series of meetings of the unemployed. These became larger and

larger and *Commonweal* proudly reported that out of two
hundred present at one meeting, only eight had been employed.[71]
George Adams wrote to Carpenter,

I have just come home from the café; we have had a good meeting of unemployed
over 200 and Jonathan T. provided coffee and bread for them; he did the same last
week. I think if that won't fetch 'em, nought will. We are going to have a demonstration tomorrow (Wednesday); there will be a deputation from the meeting
to the Guardians whilst they are sitting. I don't suppose anything will come
of it . . . poor devils . . . all of them so thankful for the little that was provided; one
quite an intelligent fellow got up and spoke. The feeling seems to be that they won't
go into the workhouse, they have to saw and cut weights of wood and chop it: and
all they get is $11\frac{1}{2}$d – no food with it.[72]

The deputation to the mayor demanding relief outside the
workhouse was followed by several open air mass meetings early in
December at West Bar, overflowing into Paradise Square. When a
meeting was held at the café, there were hundreds who could not
get in and unemployed men came in all the time with their name and
trade written on slips of paper.[73]

The socialists were as surprised as anyone else at the success
of their campaign. M.A.Maloy addressed a 'large and intelligent
audience' on 'Force no Remedy' for forty minutes; whether the
audience which took part in the discussion that followed, thought it
was or it wasn't is not clear.[74] Poor George Hukin found himself in
a great whirl of meetings and unable to go on his walks with Fannie
or have tea and play cards with the Adams or Louisa Usher.[75]
Louisa Usher must have been rarely at home. George Adams
reported to Carpenter:

Poor Mrs Usher is in a bad way just now. Old Usher is on the run again; he was at
the Café last night as drunk as a fiddler's bitch: she did cry, he says if she won't
give up coming to our meetings he will never be sober, the pig.[76]

Old Usher was to have a drunken few years if he kept his promise,
for Louisa Usher continued to be politically active.

The agitation had some effect; the Sheffield Guardians gave
out-relief and established Children's Scattered Homes so children

could be cared for outside the workhouse.[77] Jonathan Taylor's generosity was remembered too with affectionate gratitude. When better times returned to Sheffield, the daily soup and bread he had provided for two hundred of the unemployed was repaid. He was presented with a cheque and a fur-lined coat.[78]

Perhaps success took the steam out of the campaign, for the socialists were back in the doldrums in the spring of '88. Attendance at the café was declining. George Hukin was disappointed when they gave out over a thousand handbills advertising a talk by Raymond Unwin and hardly anyone came. In March 1888 he was forced to the conclusion that they would have to give up the café:

I think the town is overrun with Coffee Shops really. Don't you think it would be better to just get a room and not mix it up with any business? There are plenty of struggling shop-keepers without us adding another to the list.[79]

Carpenter agreed that the café would be regarded as 'quite a success from the propagandist point of view' but the area round Scotland Street was so poor hardly anyone could afford to buy food or coffee in the café and it was a financial failure. Carpenter was not personally sad that the café closed because he had been living in an attic at the top of the house for most of the year of the Commonwealth's existence. Up there he was almost high enough to miss the smells from the street below but exposed to soot, dirt and pollution. It was an incongruous environment for a follower of Walt Whitman and the author of *Towards Democracy*:

In the early morning at 5 a.m. there was the strident sound of the 'hummers' and the clattering of innumerable clogs of men and girls going to their work, and on till late at night there were drunken cries and shouting. Far around stretched nothing but factory chimneys and foul courts inhabited by the wretched workers.[80]

At least his harmonium playing and all those singing rehearsals in the Commonwealth had a lasting result – he spent his spare time putting together *Chants of Labour – A Song Book of the People*, with songs by Morris, Maguire, Joynes, Glasier and

Carpenter amongst others. 'It was a queer experience, collecting these songs of hope and enthusiasm and composing such answering tunes and harmonies as I could, in the midst of these gloomy and discordant conditions.'[81]

But the café did provide a focus for their activity and a place to meet and talk informally as well as listen to speeches. John Furniss, Jonathan Taylor, Thomas Garbutt, Louisa Usher, Raymond Unwin, George and Lucy Adams, Fannie and George Hukin, would all be in and out amidst the smells and noise. The Sheffield journalist, Harold Armytage, author of *Chantrey Lane*, remembered nearly half a century later how he 'saw Havelock Ellis there, and one afternoon . . . had tea at one of the little tables in this old debtors jail with Prince Kropotkin, the Russian scholar and reformer. Mrs Annie Besant and others spoke in the upper room designed for public meetings.'[82]

During 1888 such openness to a variety of radical, socialist and anarchist ideas could still survive. The politics of the socialists in Sheffield had come from such different places they could accept their diverse visitors, continue to read *Justice* as well as *Commonweal*, incline towards Mahon's North of England Socialist Federation or to the Socialist Union, an early breakaway from the SDF, with support in Bristol and Nottingham, and retain their autonomy as a group. However, their own difficulties coincided with the mounting tensions at the centre of the League. The collapse of the Commonwealth was followed by low attendance at Unwin's talk – ironically on 'Socialism and Happiness' – and the Socialist Club was still at a low ebb in the summer of 1888. Internal conflict in the Socialist League in London had flared up again in the early summer of 1888 and Morris' politics were being overtaken by those of the anarchists. Real disagreement about how to agitate for socialism, about the role of unions, the state, and demands for legislation, were making it increasingly difficult for the League to act in a concerted manner.[83] The growth of new unionism raised the question of union agitation with a militant immediacy.

In 1888 unemployment began to fall. Two boom years were to follow with an upsurge in the organisation of unskilled and semi-skilled workers. Gas-workers, dockers and women in unorganised casual work went on strike and joined unions for the first time. This 'new unionism' also affected workers in scattered crafts threatened by machinery who needed the support of a big union: quarrymen, ore miners, some of the knife and small metal trades, coopers and cement workers. The conservatism of the Friendly Society of Operative Iron-Founders left the way open for new organisations. The slogan of the 8-hour day became not just the demand of some socialists but began to have a mass impact. The miners accepted it for themselves, although it was defeated by the TUC in 1889.[84]

Though the socialists in Sheffield did take part in these developments, they were not really central to them. This was partly because of their tendency to dismiss trade union agitation, their suspicion of the demand for legislation from the state for the 8 hour day, and because the dispute between anarchists and socialists sympathetic to Morris' socialism had reached Sheffield by 1889. But it was also because of the particular structure of industry in the South Yorkshire and Derbyshire region. The scattered nature of the metal trades, sub-contracting and arbitration meant that the new unionism could not gain such dramatic support as it did among dockers or the semi-skilled labourers in the gas industry. Also the miners' organisation in Derbyshire and South Yorkshire was still deeply enmeshed in liberal politics and their leaders committed to gains through conciliation. It was not until 1893 that wage reductions and a lockout produced a near insurrection among rank and file miners in the Sheffield area.[85]

The Sheffield socialists were still in the little world they had created for themselves from the mid '80s. Unwin lectured on the sexual theorist, James Hinton, in January 1889 and 'Sketchley did all the opposition'. Unwin fell ill and could not do his follow up lecture on Hinton. But there was not a great deal of interest. 'We have had wretched meetings – not more than a dozen at either' Hukin told Carpenter. He was bothered about whether to get someone to fill in and toying with Unwin's titles 'Hinton's Ethics', or 'Evolution in Morals' or 'Licence, Restraint and Liberty'.

Carpenter must have racked his brains for a popular issue and probably remembering his experience in the attic in Scotland Street suggested a public meeting on the smoke. Hukin duly proposed this but no one was 'very keen'. Jonathan Taylor showed mild interest and Hukin rather hopelessly said he'd try to see Mrs Gilchrist, a friend of Carpenter's who was a Whitman enthusiast, and see what she thought.[86]

In July Hukin set out to visit the grinding wheels workshops in search of razor grinders in an attempt to unionise the men. Carpenter had been in London a few months earlier with a friend who was a razor grinder – almost certainly Hukin – who was giving evidence on sweating.[87] A Select Committee had been set up in 1888. But George Hukin does not appear to have been supported in his attempts at unionisation by the other members of the society. His exasperation at the political confusion they were feeling in the summer of 1889 comes out in his criticism of Robert Bingham. He had been 'told that R.B. proposed that we join the League or the SDF become a branch of one or the other. I suppose they mean I am to call a meeting of all the members to decide it. What do you think about it? I think I shall try to get R.B. to be secretary, I'm getting tired of these weekly meetings – he simply spoils everything. He first of all goes in strong for one thing – say the 8-hour day – and just when you think the meeting is going to settle about what's to be done, he suddenly remembers that after all the 8 hours is only a palliative and it is doubtful whether it's worth our while to bother about it and starts off then (and there is no stopping him) with all sorts of arguments in favour of leaving the 8-hour movement to the trade unionists. The only thing worth our while to do is to get all capital nationalised? Now what can you make of such a chap?'[88]

Hukin's irritation with Robert Bingham's political instability was partly the impatience of a behind-the-scenes organiser with the flashy orator who went for the emotional drama of the moment and never bothered to follow his enthusiasms through. Hukin, quiet, shy and conscientious, who thought before he spoke, carried burdens of responsibility and longed for peace and serenity, was quite visibly affronted by Bingham's capacity to hurtle himself publicly into contradictory positions.

But the confusion Robert Bingham expressed, the desire for some certainty, was a deeper political difference. The disputes at the centre of the League and the rise of new unionism and the 8-hour agitation made them practical choices rather than discussion points. Hukin could live politically in the gentle ambiguity of Carpenter's ambiance. He trusted Carpenter for ideas on what to do, was less concerned about principle than with following a course of action consistently. He disliked personal and political conflict intensely but had a knack of getting in the middle of it. And he was tired after more than three years of intensive political activity, emotional problems and his work.

The attraction of the anarchists was that they appeared to have clear answers and seemed uncompromising and pure. From the summer of 1889 they were increasingly setting the pace of political activity and defining the tone of militancy in the society. New names appear in the reports to *Commonweal* between August and December 1889. There is Mowbray, an anarchist from London, travelling up to speak. Fred Charles, an idealistic young anarchist who even when unemployed gave away everything he owned, came to Sheffield. There were more outdoor meetings, including ones for workers in the large ironworks which were just developing on a large scale. The Sheffield and District General Labourers Union was formed. The anarchist-communists believed it could avoid the snarl of short term economism by being explicitly a revolutionary union. It appears to have had a brief existence. However, by the end of 1889 there had been a definite shift in the politics of the Sheffield Socialist Club. Carpenter was already remote from this industrial activity and busy with his speaking outside Sheffield and no longer a pivot of the society. In London, Morris remained mysteriously silent. The original nucleus had split. Drury, Hukin, Adams, Taylor and Mrs Maloy were on the sidelines. The Bingham brothers and Louisa Usher were drawing closer to the anarchists. The peculiar amalgam of radicalism, utopian communitarianism, marxism and ethical socialism which had formed the basis of the society was being superseded by a politics of confrontation, direct action and a resurgent enthusiasm that revolution was just around the corner.

In 1890 Carpenter went away to Ceylon and India. Meditating with an Eastern religious teacher he was completely removed from developments in the Sheffield Socialist Club. Events moved swiftly after the arrival of the fiery Irish doctor John Creaghe who brought links with international anarchism. He had been involved in Argentina with anarchist exiles from Spain and Italy.

Towards the end of 1890 Morris finally broke with the anarchist-communists in the Socialist League. There was no longer any restraint on the calls for blood and dynamite in *Commonweal* edited by David Nicoll. The local politics of the Sheffield anarchists reflected this shift and the violent rhetoric escalated. George Hukin became increasingly estranged from the club. He rarely went down there while Carpenter was away during 1890 and 1891. But the anarchists for whom militancy and illegality were synonymous continued their whirl of activity. Bingham was charged with inciting strikers at Browns to attack blacklegs and his trial dragged on. Creaghe started a 'No Rent Strike' in 1891. This meant he refused to pay his landlady rent, fought off police and bailiffs and waited for the movement to spread. It did not. A French anarchist Coulon visited Sheffield and helped Fred Charles to set up a paper. *The Sheffield Anarchist* ('pay what you like') exhorted people to take similar forms of direct action. However, by the end of the year the paper had collapsed and even John Creaghe had to admit failure. Much worse was to come. In February 1892 Fred Charles was arrested with a group of other anarchists. Coulon, who had persuaded them to make a plan for a bomb, was in fact a police spy. The sentences were severe, regardless of the evidence of police provocation. Charles was sentenced to ten years. Carpenter was to be involved in an uneasy alliance with David Nicoll in a long and unsuccessful struggle to get Charles' sentence reduced. The Walsall bomb incident left the Sheffield Socialist Club demoralised and divided.

Ironically, in the summer of 1893 there were widespread colliery riots against a reduction in wages. The insurrection had occurred – but a little late. Police and troops were marched to the Sheffield area. Lord Rosebery intervened between men and employers. It was the first direct involvement of the state in the guise of mediator between labour and capital.[89]

### The Socialist Movement and a Culture of Everyday Life

Although there were quite particular radical traditions which helped to shape the socialist movement in Sheffield, their ways of organising and their debates and controversies were by no means unique. News travelled not only through the movement's papers like *Commonweal* but also through speakers visiting different towns and through friends. Carpenter travelled all over Britain as a speaker from the 1880s to the 1900s. In *My Days and Dreams* he says he 'spoke and lectured in the Socialist connection'[90] all around the country – at Bradford, Halifax, Leeds, Glasgow, Dundee, Edinburgh, Hull, Liverpool, Nottingham.

Local propaganda exchanges made obvious sense. There were links among the Midlands socialists and anarchists in the 1880s for example which continued despite splits in London. Sheffield and Chesterfield were particularly close because of the old friendship with Raymond Unwin in Chesterfield. In June 1889 Carpenter wrote to the Glaswegian socialist tailor, James Brown, saying that he and Jim Shortland,

went (with a bicycle between us) to Chesterfield for an evening meeting in the market-place. There is a navvy there – Andrew Hall – a regular rough looking chap, who lives in a common lodging house, who speaks on Soc^m [sic] every Sunday evg. [sic]. He has read a *lot*, history and all sorts and speaks well. There was an attentive audience of 400 to 500. I made a little speech and Shortland sang one or two songs.[91]

The special observation of Hall as a labourer is interesting. Most of the socialists appear to have been small independent tradesmen or workers in old craft occupations, many of which were in decline. Jim Shortland was another exception, working at the big iron works of Vickers and Maxims. Carpenter described him as 'handsome, fiery and athletic, an engine-fitter always ready for a row and to act as "chucker-out" if required'.[92]

The friendship, the bicycle for local propaganda and the importance of song were characteristic of the socialist movement then. The speaker was an important propaganda asset, especially a speaker with a loud voice. For this kind of socialism the main thing was to *make* socialists; it was less important quite what kind. The response was frequently far from enthusiastic.

Carpenter had close friendship links with Leeds which dated back to Isabella Ford in University Extension days. Towards the end of the 1880s, the organisation of unskilled and semi-skilled workers in the Leeds area meant that Leeds socialists, Isabella Ford, Tom Maguire and Alf Mattison were deeply involved in organising tailors, tailoresses and gas-workers, but this came after several years of apparently fruitless propaganda. Carpenter describes joint propaganda outings to the villages of South Yorkshire and Derbyshire:

Many a time we have gone down to some mining village and taken up our stand on some heap of slag or broken wall, and the miners would come round and stand about or sit down deliberately *with their backs to the speaker*, and spit, and converse, as if quite heedless of the oration going on.

If they kept going long enough they would start to listen with interest but not the country people. Even the wit and charm of Maguire failed at Hathersage in Derbyshire. 'We set him up on a stone heap in the middle of the village and standing round him ourselves while he spoke, acted as decoy ducks to bring the villagers together.'

But their audience stayed out of hearing and simply stared, ignoring the socialists attempts to persuade them to come nearer.

In vain the speaker shouted himself hoarse and fired off his best jokes. Not a bit of it – they weren't going to be fooled by us! and at last red in the face and out of breath and with a string of curses, Tom descended from his cairn, and we all, shaking the dust of the village off our feet, departed.[93]

Because they were so isolated there was a corresponding stress on internal fellowship among the early socialists. Years later Alf Mattison remembered his frequent visits to Millthorpe when he was out of work. The part the cottage played as a kind of social centre for socialists, anarchists, mystics and free-thinkers was recognisable in a socialist milieu which had a whole network of such centres in different forms. Harry Snell, a Nottingham socialist, remembered a Sunday fellowship meeting at Ambergate, a mid-way stop between Sheffield, Nottingham and Leicester where they 'crowded into a local inn where Carpenter played the piano and we sang the best-known Socialist Songs'.[94]

Music was an important element in this personal comradeship and Carpenter's *England Arise* became one of their favourites. It was a means of binding together small groups who were pitted against the world outside but more than this the early socialists saw music, poems and the artistry of their banners as the beginnings of a new culture.

Carpenter had particularly long and close links with Bristol which is a good example of the strengths of this kind of socialism. The radical connection went back to his friendship with Riley who had lived and propagandised there in the 1890s. There was a whole family of Sharland brothers who were his friends, Robert Gilliard and a Christian socialist workman called Robert Weare, as well as women socialists, Helena Born, Miriam Daniell, Kate St John Conway. In Bristol the activities and ideas of the socialists resemble the Sheffield club quite closely and, like Sheffield, Bristol was an autonomous group which did not belong to any organisation. The national links and influences thus came informally.

Music and art were as essential for the rituals of organising as the open air meeting. One of the earliest minutes of the Bristol socialists records that readings, recitations and music were introduced 'As Socialism was a movement inspired by art as well as of economics.'[95]

As the Sharland brothers were a musical family they used to sing at meetings:

At that date very few socialist songs had been written, although songs of Liberty, Freedom, and True Brotherhood were in plenty, but with rare exceptions no music for either had been composed. Will Sharland got over this by slightly varying the existing words to existing melodies, or re-casting and adapting some accompaniment and arrangement of old and standard airs to fit the words.[96]

This work was acknowledged in Carpenter's preface to *Chants of Labour* in 1888, which included songs by Carpenter himself, Havelock Ellis, Henry Salt, Jim Joynes, Bruce Glasier, Walt Whitman and David Nicoll. Later the Bristol socialists produced their own songbook for which J. Percival Jones, a Bristol workman, composed tunes.

The culture of early socialism invoked more than art. It involved the creation of new forms for all aspects of people's lives. It had to provide a kind of home for people made spiritually homeless in capitalism. On Michaelmas Day, 1887, the Bristol socialists held a tea and social evening. This was the beginning of a whole series of teas, dances and theatrical entertainments which included not only the men who up to then had been the main propagandists, but women and children too. One Bristol socialist, Robert Gilliard, commented on the antagonism which women had felt to the political activity of the men which kept them out late. There were 'black looks' when the weary socialist husbands returned and the women resentfully complained 'it is the same every night, Sunday and weekday alike'. It was evident that conflict in the family would weaken adherence to the movement. But after the involvement of the women and children in the social events everyone was out late and nobody could complain. 'Thus we won our families over to the cause, and with them their most valuable help.'[97]

The involvement of women was not only a matter of organisational efficiency. In Bristol socialism implied also a new position for women and change in relations between the sexes. In part this came out of the emphasis on personal change and the creation of new forms for everyday life. The influence of Whitman and Carpenter was important and also the activity of a group of women within the society, Miriam Daniell, Helena Born, Kate Conway and Enid Stacy, as well as the upsurge of trade union militancy among women workers. Among the talks to the Bristol Socialist Society in 1889 were 'Why women should organise and the aristocracy of sex' by Helena Born and 'Evolution of Women' by Miriam Daniell. Helena Born believed in democracy in sexual relations. Like Carpenter, she urged women to have faith in freedom. She thought the oppression of women was irrevocably bound to the position of men in capitalism: 'Whatever degrades one member of a sex degrades all, and an insult offered to one sex is an insult to both.'[98] Both women and men would have to change: 'Genuine comradeship is possible only if the man becomes effeminate or when the woman to some extent rationalises her costume.'[99]

'Comradeship' was not an abstract term but a personal relationship for the ethical socialists. One of the Bristol socialists who knew Born and Daniell said of their friendship.

If we ever meet Miriam in the spiritual world she will have her arms round Helena's neck and declare that she was the dearest friend, the most helpful companion, the one who understood her best – and Helena will not believe it.[100]

A neighbour and fellow socialist said of the Bristol socialists, 'Whitman sings beautifully of loving comrades but his verses do not begin to touch upon the real delight of the actual bliss of comradeship in practice'.[101] There was an intensity of feeling in fellowship and comradeship which was not limited to relations in Bristol. Glasier, writing of James Brown, referred particularly to the Whitmanic love of comrades which was such an important aspect of the movement. While Alf Mattison wrote to the historian of the Social Democratic Federation, H.W.Lee, saying he thought that he should stress personal fellowship as an aspect of the history more.[102]

New forms of relationship were seen as part of the practice of socialism – so was a deliberately chosen alternative style of life.

Born and Daniell lived in a small house in a working-class area of Bristol where, like Carpenter,

they set an example of practical simplicity in household matters showing aesthetic possibilities in colour and ingenious and artistic adaptation which was a revelation to their neighbours. With their own hands they tinted the walls of their rooms and waxed the uncarpeted floors, while from the most commonplace materials they improvised many articles of furniture and decoration, combining both beauty and utility.[103]

When Edward Carpenter came to lecture in Bristol, Helena Born made the floor shine with 'beeswax, turps and "elbow-grease" and hoped no visitors would call before he came bringing in mud from the streets outside'.[104] 'Simplification of life' did not always remove the need for hard work.

This alternative way of life bordered on bohemianism. Helena Born chose her own kind of clothes. Simplicity for both her and Miriam Daniell was a feature of their standards of dress, house furnishing as well as of their 'tastes and habits'.[105] Unconventionality did not isolate them from other socialists. One of their Bristol comrades reflected, 'no amount of kicking over the traces seemed to affect our regard for her, except to increase it'.[106] Funny clothes and funny ideas about sexual freedom were also not restricted to the Bristol socialists. Bruce Glasier on his early propaganda tours presented an extraordinary appearance: 'Free and un-conventional in dress and manner, a disreputable hat crowning his shaggy locks, a picturesque cloak for wet weather.'[107]

When Glasier met and wooed Kate St John Conway she expressed a similar impatience with convention, sending her lover questions about his views on a wife. 'What does a poet think of a woman with ink on her finger and a hole in her stocking. What would he say to two *thick* ankles? . . . What would he say to a woman who would sooner eat bread and butter and drink milk or buy fruit for dinner than cook it. . . . Again, what would a poet say to a woman who *liked* earning money and enjoyed the thought of being a breadwinner as well as wife that the husband might *never* have to sell even a hair of himself?'[108]

They were married according to Scottish common law by declaration before two witnesses. The custom of retaining both names in a democratic union brought a joking note from Carpenter saying he was concerned 'with the convolutions of your future joint name – Mr and Mrs Katharine Bruce St John Conway-Glasier or Glasier Conway seems something like it ought to be'.[109]

Katharine St John Conway was teaching classics at Redland High School in Bristol and became a socialist in the wave of militant trade unionism which swept the town between 1889–90. Helena Born and Miriam Daniell, with other socialists, helped to organise the cotton operatives who came out on strike in October 1889. On Sunday mornings the strikers in clean white aprons and shawls over their heads marched to the churches and chapels. Robert Weare led one group to the All Saints Church, Clifton. They went into the church and stood between the altar rails and the congregation, wet and bedraggled because it was raining. The young classics teacher, steeped in high church ethics and conscious of her intellectual superiority as a Newnham graduate, was so moved she went next day to the dingy socialist coffee house in the Old Rope Walk. She was received with reserve as a middle class young lady. She said later that she deserved such a reception, conscious of the need to maintain her respectability and 'the special privilege of the Anglo-Catholic communion'. But she was dismayed when one of the socialists took down Francis Adams' *Songs of the Armies of the Night* from the shelves and showed her a biting poem 'A Pretty Little Lady who has Lost her Way'. When 'a tall gentle workman', the Christian Socialist, Robert Weare, intervened to say 'Give her Carpenter's *England's Ideal* that is what she needs' she was instinctively grateful.[110]

'"Who is Carpenter?" I asked. For the group who gathered round us the answer absorbed the rest of the evening.'[111] Becoming a socialist amounted to a religious conversion as Kate Conway said 'For many of us inside and outside the political Socialist movement . . . Walt Whitman's *Leaves of Grass* and Edward Carpenter's

*Towards Democracy* had become a modern bible.'[112] She read
*England's Ideal* late into the night after talking to the Bristol
socialists.

As I went back to my Clifton lodgings I vaguely realised that every value life
had previously held for me had been changed as by some mysterious alchemy. I
was ashamed of the privileges and elaborate refinements of which I had previously
been so proud. The joy of companionship, the glory of life lost and found, the 'age
long peerless cause' had been revealed to me, dimming all others.[113]

Despite the immense differences between the lives of
working-class and middle-class women the upsurge of new
unionism provided a real association for a short time.

For Helena Born and Miriam Daniell 1889–90 was a
strenuous autumn and winter. An American friend, Helen Tufts,
wrote later, 'through their incessant efforts funds were gathered
from all parts of the country in aid of the strike of the Bristol cotton
operatives. Night upon night, after days of unremitting activity,
into the small hours they sat counting the pennies taken up at local
meetings and strike parades and planning the judicious disburse-
ment of the money among the needy strikers.'[114] Though a
feminist Helena Born believed in the need for men and women
workers to organise together rather than in separate unions. She
explained to a friend in the Women's Liberal Association that the
gas workers union was 'one of the few unions initiated by men
which accords women full representation on its councils, and has
included among its objects obtaining, wherever possible, the same
wages for women doing the same work as men'.[115]

Early in 1890 Helena Born tried to organise the sweated
seamstresses, many of whom worked at home. She wrote to her
cousin saying she had two or three meetings a night.[116] The women
were scattered all around Bristol. They worked extremely long
hours for very low pay. The organisation of workers in this
situation presented tremendous difficulties. Tufts describes how
Helena Born might have to tramp thirty miles in a day, 'scouring
the country on her self-imposed mission'.[117] She succeeded in

recruiting the women by this effort but because the women carried home work and had little contact with one another the union consisted of isolated and passive members and they did not find a means of acting effectively together.

Carpenter was remote from this industrial organising which involved his friends. E.P.Thompson in *Homage to Tom Maguire* describes him watching events in Leeds with awe but without any advice to offer his comrades. In the midst of the new union struggles he was writing to Alf Mattison about Havelock Ellis' book, *The New Spirit*, which included a study of Whitman. The young engineer might well have wondered whether *The New Spirit* had any ideas on how to fight Gas Company employers and the Leeds liberal establishment. Carpenter, removed from such mundane tactical considerations, viewed political upheaval in cosmic terms.

'Everything seems to be rushing on faster and faster. Where are we going? Niagara, or the Islands of the Blest?'[118] Carpenter's response indicates a more general weakness in the socialism of the 1880s which had serious consequences. It meant there was a gap between the internal organisation of club and fellowship and workers' struggles outside. There was a socialist culture which often reflected the values of workers in forms of production which were being overtaken by large scale industry, or of small tradesmen, or perhaps non-conformist ministers who carried still an older tradition of radical dissent in which there was a concept of 'the people' but not of the working class. This culture was remote from most workers' lives. When the unskilled and semi-skilled organised in the late 1880s and early '90s the two merged briefly. But the effects of this on the socialist movement varied from town to town and the mass involvement could not be sustained.

In Sheffield the arrival of the anarchists and especially of the anarchist doctor, John Creaghe, the escalation of militant rhetoric, crowd violence and the Walsall bomb affair presented an especially acute crisis which accentuated this isolation. But the problem was more general for socialists in or near the League who had put such a stress on making socialists, changing consciousness. The anarchist communists merely pushed some of the already existing internal political conditions to extremes. When the Socialist League collapsed in 1892 it marked a shift in socialist politics which was reflected in the formation of the more firmly based but not revolutionary ILP.

Nonetheless these early socialists had also great strengths. If their ethical idealism made some dismissive of class conflict and trade union agitation it also made them very grand about what they wanted. It was evident to them that socialism meant not just a redistribution of wealth, not even the workers owning and controlling production. Socialism had to bring a transformation of all human relationships, not just at work but in everyday life – including socialist meetings. They were able to talk about happiness and love and the new life as part of becoming a socialist. Political commitment implied an internal change. The anarchists presented the most extreme version of this for Creaghe and his comrades, the distinction between subjective feeling and objective possibility was lost and the revolution started from the moment someone became an anarchist. But among revolutionary socialists like Maguire, Born and Daniells there was an understanding tempered with more tactical sense of the interaction between external political action and personal feeling. Carpenter's continuing struggle in both his writing and his life to connect the two was thus part of a wider context. Indeed it was possible for him to assume that such connections were possible because he belonged to a movement in which many people shared a common structure of feeling. They did not need to assert the importance of creating a personal culture of everyday life as a means of resisting capitalism because they took it for granted. They did not make priorities of different forms of activity so it did not occur to them to reduce socialism to a struggle for economic power.

They knew they wanted not only a society in which there would be no exploitation but much more a society where everyone could create and in which life was beautiful. Morris, Carpenter and Unwin wrote and spoke of this socialism which by changing the conditions of labour and creating new forms of community would make possible a closer and more harmonious relationship to the external world. They wanted things to be made for need and not for profit. They wanted to democratise beauty and transform the texture of living. They sought to live out something of this future in the here and now. In reality they did not of course always live up to what they wanted. Tom Maguire, who was really an embodiment of these politics, a poet, an organiser of unskilled workers in his early twenties, a witty and eloquent speaker, able to notice the most intimate details in personal behaviour, with a special sympathy and understanding for women workers, died still a young man, of poverty and alcohol, neglected by the Leeds socialists who were locked in internal conflicts. Before he died he noted how difficult it was to really change inside:

People call themselves Socialists but what they really are is just ordinary men with Socialist opinions hung round; they haven't got it inside them. It's hard, very hard; we get mixed up in disputes among ourselves . . . and can't keep a straight line for the great thing, even if we all of us know what that is.[119]

Well they missed the 'great thing' these small bands of comrades. But they made briefly a movement in which a total vision of socialism could emerge as a challenge to all the distortions which capitalism brought to social relations. The vision did not become reality and this left the romantic socialism of the 1880s and early '90s a remote and broken tradition. Much of their hope was overwhelmed in disappointment, weariness and disillusion by the late 1890s when the old world went on its own way and utopia was whittled away by the everyday. Although some of the old campaigners, including Carpenter, were still at it in the 1900s many had been scattered.

Even in the mid 1890s there was a feeling that an era had ended. On Easter Saturday 1895, Carpenter, Mattison and Shortland went on a propaganda ramble handing out leaflets, but there was a sadness and consciousness of absence about the excursion. Tom Maguire had died, impossible not to remember him shaking the dust from his feet when the country people refused to listen. Fred Charles was in prison and all their efforts at reprieve had been a failure.[120] Charles' fate was the grim side to that heady utopianism which had confused the world as it was with the world as they wanted it to be.

Capitalism has several means of dealing with its opponents; either it absorbs them – Glasier became Ramsay MacDonald's henchman; Unwin designed garden cities – or it dashes them to pieces like Tom Maguire. Some it drove to seek a new world across the Atlantic or Pacific Oceans. Helena Born and Miriam Daniell went to live together in America where it seemed as if there was more scope for the new life. Another Bristol socialist, Robert Allan Nicoll, went to a utopian colony in California. John Furniss emigrated to farm in New Zealand.

This romantic or ethical socialism is difficult to define because it was congenitally vague. Briefly in the 1880s and early 1890s, it combined its vision of how the world should be with the struggle against exploitation. Its influence was important in the Socialist League and in the autonomous socialist groups. Despite the opposition of the SDF leadership it was not without effect at a local branch level. Carpenter was a key figure, linking socialists with men and women who were seeking a new way of life. It was not that ethical socialism was a political tendency directed from Millthorpe. It was rather that Carpenter's break with the Christian faith, his search for an alternative harbour for the soul, his consciousness of sexual and social fragmentation was experienced more generally by his contemporaries. They saw in him a kind of prophet rather than a political leader. He seemed to live their own dilemma. Carpenter's later writing in the 1890s about sexual liberation came very naturally from these politics. But he began to explore sexual questions when the movement which carried the connection between personal change and socialist revolution was beginning to wane.

Ethical socialism did not abruptly expire with the organisational collapse of the Socialist League because it was an approach to politics rather than a conscious ideology. But it changed. Although socialists like Maguire and Mattison carried it into the early Independent Labour Party, the connection with revolutionary socialism was really lost with the defeat of Morris and the disintegration of the Socialist League. From the mid 1890s ethical socialism belonged increasingly to socialists who had abandoned hope of revolution. But it remained quite distinct from the more utilitarian social reformism of the Fabians. The importance of the club, the stress on fellowship, the bicycle outings, the songs, poems, music and love, the everyday culture which bound men and women to the movement continued in the Clarion movement, the Independent Labour Party and later the Labour Party. Ethical socialism continued to be a living force certainly until the 1920s. It was, however, a culture contained by its dependence on a politics which sought power within the terms of capitalism. The creation of the Labour Party merely institutionalised this dependence. The ethical socialist was for ever waiting in limbo. The ideal belonged to the long term. In the short term there was the immediate compromise. Thus the passionate opposition to Mrs Grundy had to be held in check by the need not to frighten potential supporters. Utopia had to be tidied away in a dusty cupboard; the last item on an agenda which was somehow never reached.

### Personal and Sexual Relations with Men

Carpenter's writing on sexual liberation and socialism grew not only out of a movement which assumed an interaction of personal and public but also from his own intense and often painful attempt to relate honestly to men and women who were not of his class. He wanted to love more openly and less possessively. Millthorpe was the outer symbol of this inner practice. He wrote *Towards Democracy, England's Ideal, Desirable Mansions* in his garden hut by the brook at Millthorpe and tried to combine this with manual labour, growing produce with the stolidly uncommercial Albert Fearnehough and taking it to market. Around 1887–88 the demands of writing combined with political activity meant that he was forced to hand over the business side of the market garden to Fearnehough.

Millthorpe, with its quiet rhythm of manual work, writing, music, talk, sunbaths and visits to the pub, became a centre for both middle-class socialists and radicals like the Salts, Olive Schreiner, G. Lowes Dickinson and later E.M.Forster, Havelock Ellis and Edith Lees, and for workers like Alf Mattison and Sheffield friends, George Hukin, Jim Shortland, James Brown, George and Lucy Adams, who lived with Carpenter after the Fearnehoughs went, as well as for an increasing body of eccentric visitors who tramped for several miles from the railway station to observe 'simplification of life'.

Carpenter wanted Millthorpe to act as a place where all classes met and distinction dissolved. It was characteristic of his socialism to hope to transcend the actual with the ideal. It is not to dismiss the importance of Millthorpe for its visitors to say that the reality was sometimes more uncomfortable than he might admit. The actual inequalities of class and sex persisted however much his politics attempted to overcome differences. There was also a necessary self-consciousness in his attempt to break with the details, still so significant, of his class. Charles Sixsmith, his Whitmanite friend from Bolton, observed of Carpenter's 'reaction from gentility and respectability' that:

He would laugh at a coarse joke but never tell one, and an odd time would use an oath but it seemed forced and unnatural in him. There were still traces left of his early curate days and his unconventionality was partly acquired and deliberate.[121]

The awkwardness went both ways. George Hukin who was a close comrade and dear friend felt 'mean and little' beside Carpenter at first:

I know you have always tried to put me at my ease to make me feel at home with you. Sorry I cannot come nearer to you. How I should like! Yet I feel I can't. . . . Forgive me for calling you Mr, I know I've offended you by doing so. I won't do again I assure you.[122]

When Alf Mattison was victimised because of his part in the organisation of the gasworkers in Leeds, Carpenter gave sympathy and help but there was nonetheless a real class difference in their predicament. He had a private income, he could go to Italy when he

was weary with politics, he could go to India and Ceylon and
practise yoga peacefully with a Gnani. For working-class socialists
no such respite and renewal was possible.

Henry Salt, who had a mischievous tendency to poke fun at
Edward Carpenter's prophetic aspect – perhaps because of Kate
Salt's hopeless love for Carpenter – wrote teasingly:

> *To Edward Carpenter in Ceylon*
> O'er Ceylon's Isle the spicy breezes
> Blow soft, while torpid Britain freezes.
> Gay Bard of Brotherhood is't fair?
> We shivering here, you basking there?
> Is this your *Towards Democracy*?
> Are we your freeborn comrades – we,
> Left wondering thus, like spirits lost,
> In purgatorial fog and frost,
> While you sit calm, 'neath summer skies
> On Adam's Peak in Adam's guise.[123]

There was also a personal charisma about Carpenter which
drew people to him very directly and non-verbally but which also
ultimately distanced him. He became a being apart, carrying some
guru-like qualities which must have strained his spirit. Alf
Mattison, for instance, describes meeting him at a socialist meeting
in Leeds in 1889. The physical and emotional effect of the
encounter remained with him very vividly years later. 'Therefore
when he shook my hand, I instantly thrilled at the touch. No
words can adequately express my feelings in those first moments
of my contact with his magnetic personality.'[124] Charlie Sixsmith
describes being similarly drawn to him[125] but again Henry Salt
dismissed the idea of Carpenter as possessing any spiritual power.
Far from being calm and detached he described Carpenter as being
agitated underneath and torn by internal conflict.[126] It is likely that
Carpenter's ability to communicate without words depended very
much on the responsiveness of whoever he was with.

There were, however, very good reasons for him to experience
strain and conflict. He was after all trying to live out a new way of

life which challenged not only the relationship between the classes but was sexually unorthodox. He was under great pressure as a local activist, a speaker and writer. Moreover, his loving relationships were fraught and unhappy until he met George Merrill and even then they were unable to live together for some years.

After his initial interest in Joe Potter, the young man who used to run in the races before he went to sea as a marine engineer, he developed a relationship with George Hukin just as the socialist group was forming. It was a painful love for Carpenter, not only because of George Hukin's feelings of class-distance and self-hatred but because Hukin was already involved with Fannie who was to become his wife. The struggle of the two men to relate honestly comes through in their letters, a rare clear cameo of considerable courage.

Hukin wrote in May 1887 of a talk they had had in bed and of his relief to be able to tell Carpenter about Fannie. 'Oh how often I had wanted to tell you about it – ever since that first night I slept with you at Millthorpe. You don't know how miserable I have felt all along, just because I wanted to tell you, and yet somehow I was afraid to. But I shall not be afraid to tell you anything in future if you will only let me.' He assured Carpenter that he missed him much more than he thought he should 'and I don't find it so nice sleeping alone as I used to think it was'.[127]

But he was overwhelmingly in love with Fannie. They were staying in alone together in the evenings and going for walks along Queen's Road.[128] 'But don't think we have forgotten you, dear Ted, for if we didn't [sic] both of us love you so much, I don't think we should love each other as much as we do. I'm sure we both love *you* more than ever Ted, and you really must come and live with us when we do marry.'[129] There is of course love and love and Carpenter was unhappy and did not feel included in George Hukin's boundless loving. A few days later he was writing again, guilty and distraught with the old self-hatred asserting itself:

I can't bear to think that you are so unhappy and that I am the cause of it all. I sometimes think that I can never bring anything but unhappiness to either of you or Fannie and then I feel so miserable that I would like to die. Perhaps it would be best, then your wound might heal the sooner and Fannie might forget all about me then.[130]

This produced a telegram from Edward Carpenter, assurances he was happy for George and Fannie, and apologies throughout the summer from George Hukin.[131] George married Fannie that year. Carpenter symbolically gave them a bed for which Hukin was grateful because it was softer and wider than the one they had. It was so wide in fact that 'we might easily lose each other in it if it wasn't for the way it sinks in the middle, which somehow throws us together whether or no.'[132]

He still could not accept that his love for Fannie cut him off from Edward Carpenter.

I do wish you could sleep with us sometimes Ted, but I don't know whether Fannie would quite like it yet and I don't feel I would press it on her anyway. Still I often think how nice it would be if we three could only love each other so that we might sleep together sometimes without feeling that there was anything at all wrong in doing so.[133]

He had been thinking of him for whole days at work; there were many things he could not tell Carpenter about these thoughts – perhaps it was as well. Then he goes on to discuss Carpenter's 'knock in the face' on Bloody Sunday when Carpenter and Bob Muirhead scuffled with the police.[134] There is no reference to physical love in the later letters though there is the odd flirtatious remark. Their friendship survived. 'Years bring no shadow between us'. Carpenter wrote in 'Philolaus to Diocles':

> And sweeter far to suffer is it, dear one, being sometimes absent,
> Than (if indeed 'twere possible) to feel the opposite pain
> Of too much nearness, and love dying so
> Down to mere slackness

Instead:

> The harp is finely strung;
> A tender tension animates the strings.

His thoughts of George Hukin harmonised the wilderness. George was still with him 'Down to the roots of being' even to death. 'I shall sleep as I have slept before; so oft, in dreamless peace, close-linked with thee.'[135] George was forever comrade and lover emerging from the dusty razor-grinding workshop.[136]

Carpenter's tussle with his own feelings of jealousy must have been complicated by having a woman as a rival. The whole force of social approval was certainly with Fannie's love not his. But he did not seem to think Hukin would be threatened by his meeting an Italian boy on holiday. Both he and Hukin were already conscious of love as a non-exclusive relationship even if they could not live this in fact. Carpenter had gone a step further; he had already glimpsed that in order to sustain themselves they needed a more conscious grouping.

He wrote to his college friend, Charles Oates, in Meanwood, Leeds, in December 1887:

We are going to form by degrees a body of friends who will be tied together by the strongest general bond and also by personal attachment and that we shall help each other immensely by the mutual support we shall be able to give each other. The knowledge that there are others in the same position as oneself will remove that sense of loneliness when plunged in the society of the philistines which is almost unbearable.[137]

After Hukin was married Carpenter became involved in another triangular situation. In this case he was the interloper. He was friendly with two Glasgow Socialist Leaguers because of early propaganda activities, James Brown the tailor who moved near Millthorpe for his health in the autumn of 1890, and Bob Muirhead, a young mathematics teacher. Muirhead went to work at Cecil Reddie's progressive school, Abbotsholme in Derbyshire, in 1889, and Carpenter and he grew closer because of this proximity. At first there was enthusiasm about the school. Ashbee and Lowes Dickinson were involved and there were schemes for craft-teaching. But Muirhead and Reddie fell out and Carpenter withdrew support from the school.[138]

When Muirhead and Brown were first separated Carpenter

appears to have felt uneasy about Muirhead's neglect of his Glasgow friend. He excused Muirhead – 'he moves by laws of his own',[139] and assured James Brown, 'I keep hugging Bob for you'.[140] In January 1890 he described how beautiful he found Bob Muirhead's body and assured the anxious Brown that Muirhead had an emotional, not sexual, love for Olive Schreiner. Even if he were to marry he would miss 'that precious something wh. [sic] is only found in comradeship'.[141]

Then in March he wrote abruptly to James Brown. 'You will be surprised to hear that I slept last night with Bob – at Derby – I hope you won't be jealous. But I don't think you are. It was so good to have him. . . . He was loving and good and we did not forget you.'[142]

James Brown's feelings go unrecorded. Carpenter was defining the terms of the morality. Negligence in personal relations was embarrassing, open physical encounters with a friend were acceptable. Subsequently James Brown and Bob Muirhead appear to have drifted apart. Muirhead was attracted to Olive Schreiner and Brown became close to Jim Shortland the labourer at Vickers who nursed him through his illness. James Brown inclined to the anarchist-communists and became friendly with Fred Charles. He died early in 1893 somewhat estranged from Carpenter.

Whatever the painful inner responses there was nonetheless a startling break with conventional sexual relationships. They were crossing divides of class, gender and monogamy all at once in the midst of intense political activity, faction fights and anarchist trials. When the socialist group in Sheffield was at a low ebb after the Walsall affair, political demoralisation combined with personal disintegration. Life at Millthorpe became increasingly complicated. After the Fearnehoughs went in 1893, George and Lucy Adams moved in. At first all went well but Carpenter's relationship with George Adams deteriorated. Adams was consumed with jealousy and hatred because of Carpenter's love for George Merrill.

Carpenter first met Merrill around 1891 when he was just back from India and emotionally attuned to intense wordless communication. They exchanged 'a look of recognition'[143] in the railway carriage coming from Sheffield to Totley. Merrill followed Carpenter and they arranged to meet. It was the beginning of a lifelong relationship. For the first time, when he was already approaching middle age, Edward Carpenter found continuing sexual and emotional happiness. But this could not be fully realised until the Adams' moved out with some bitterness in 1898.

George Merrill fulfilled all Carpenter's longing for a relationship freed from the restraints of relations between men of his class. Merrill was completely remote from notions of respectability. His ignorance of the Bible must have been extraordinary to someone like Carpenter steeped in Christian culture. On hearing that Gethsemane was the garden where Jesus spent his last night, George Merrill's response was 'who with?'[144]

He had been brought up in poverty in the slums of Sheffield. His father, injured at work and permanently unemployed, drank and there was constant conflict in the family. His mother was the real force. Carpenter describes her as 'a big racy-tongued, good-hearted woman with stout voice and leg of mutton arms'.[145] There were nine children and they grew up higgledy-piggledy with little privacy. He went out to work at thirteen passing through a series of jobs, giving out towels in a baths, fetching and carrying for the moulders and casters, file grinding, driving a horse and cart, then at seventeen becoming a barman and waiter in a pub. His previous sexual experience had been in a very different world from Carpenter's small socialist body of comrades and Carpenter's description of Merrill's background gives a fascinating glimpse of the late Victorian homosexual underground. He appears to have never been attracted physically to women – though they were sometimes fond of him. At the baths there was a girl called Susan for instance, and Laura, the daughter of the pub-owners, who was a year older than him, fell in love with him: 'she began fairly spooning me . . . and trying to get round me all she could. She used to let me frizzle the bacon at breakfast, before the fire – and let the dripping fall on a bit of toast for me. She was really awfully good – and I was fond of her, but not in that way.'[146] Young Merrill liked the bacon dripping but remained indifferent to the spooning though Susan and Laura remained his friends for years. Soon after his job in the bar, he met a priest from a boys' seminary and went to wait at table until 'undue familiarities occurred'; there was a row, scandal and 'Father D.' had to go abroad hurriedly.[147] At twenty George Merrill got a job selling encyclopaedias and this travelling life brought more chance sexual contacts. He was approached by an elderly man in Scarborough when he was travelling, he met an Italian count and they used to go bathing together in the early morning. At York station, when the Prince of Wales visited, a young man in his retinue beckoned to him and arranged to meet him that evening.[148] This was the first time that Merrill's sexual feelings had any real connection to friendship. Despite the enormous class gulf and the impossibility of their love they felt great affection.

'He told me a bit about himself. He said he didn't care for the shooting and the cards and all that sort of thing. But he couldn't help himself and had to go through with it. But he did long for some real love and affection from anyone like me – only it was impossible – like in his position.'[149] The young aristocrat wanted him to come and stay in his big country house and asked him to write but Merrill lost the bit of paper with the address on it and never met him again. Quite what he would have done in such bizarre surroundings is unclear. If Merrill fulfilled all Carpenter's fantasies of direct sensuality, Carpenter's gentle affection must have been welcome, for the life of a working-class homosexual was hard and love was a chancy affair. Carpenter was most struck by 'the pathetic look of wistfulness in his face' on their first meeting. 'Whatever his experiences up to then may have been, it assured me that the desire of his *heart* was still unsatisfied.'[150]

But it took seven years from their first meeting before they could live together. Carpenter used to visit Merrill who took a cottage in Sheffield, 75 Edward Street. There were material problems on both sides. George Merrill needed to find employment. He worked for a newspaper in Sheffield, then as a waiter at a hydro nearby but lost the job in 1896. Jim Shortland got him a job at Vickers and Maxims as an unskilled labourer greasing the machines and keeping the parts clean. It was a shock after his previous work.

From evening clothes and waiting at table to corduroys and the din and uproar of a huge machine shop was certainly a great transformation. The planing by machinery of huge armour plates (for battle ships yet only half-built) went on night and day. Huge steel shavings an inch or two wide and many inches in length were licked by the great chisels off the edges of the plates as if they were so much butter. Enormous cranes and trolleys running overhead lifted the huge masses from time to time and transferred them across the vast shed. A sense of irresistible force was everywhere around. The mechanics themselves with their surly ways only added to the impression. To George, it was a little appalling and yet something in the whole situation – particularly in the solid strength and roughness of the men – attracted him.[151]

He was popular at work because his travelling life had given him a fund of jokes, quips and songs and despite the grimness of the job there was light relief. Once he fell asleep during the night shift and his workmates tied him up; on his release he had to pay a fine of drinks all round.[152] Old workshop customs like this died hard and were taken into heavy industry.

Merrill's feelings about the situation are not clear. He certainly loved Carpenter very strongly and their personal relationship was unquestioningly resolute.

It was quite a step for Carpenter to live with Merrill. Although his socialism and his life at Millthorpe made him an eccentric rebel in his own class he was still supported by a large circle of radical and socialist friends. An explicitly homosexual lifestyle narrowed the circle of people who could remain close to him. Changes in the nature of the socialist movement were to accentuate this. George Merrill was the bringer of gifts who laid down his life at his feet 'faint and ashamed'. Carpenter saw himself as the receiver taking the ruby out of the clay. But whatever Merrill gave him he risked something for his lover too. Their 'spell of life along the road together'[153] went against the grain of what was acceptable, even to Carpenter's friends. Most of his friends were hostile to their love and the choice of living openly together isolated Carpenter.[154] It must have accentuated the loneliness he wrote about in his letter some years earlier to Charles Oates and made him more dependent on the small groups mainly of men who identified with his emotions.

The arrival of Merrill was upsetting for several reasons to his friends. It disturbed them that a man should do what they regarded as woman's work about the house. Merrill's background, his frankness and robust sensuality offended the 'unco guid'. Their relationship made Carpenter's homosexuality completely explicit and unignorable.

They all said the housework would not get done. 'They drew sad pictures of the walls of my cottage hanging with cobwebs.'[155] Carpenter and Merrill both took great pride in refuting these sceptics. Characteristically Carpenter felt George did not merely do a woman's work as well as any woman, but he transformed the whole nature of housework into a creative activity – he made it an 'artistic pleasure'.[156] They both took a delight in confounding women with Merrill's skill. Tom Barclay, a Leicester anarchist, describes visiting Millthorpe with Archibald Gorrie, a socialist who took photographs and hearing from George Merrill that when he was 'in an upstairs room with the window open he heard two women talking to one another as they came along the lane underneath':

'there isn't a woman about the place I tell you' said one. 'But who's polished this, and who's scrubbed the other and who's cleaned all those?' 'I popped my head out of the window', said Merrill and replied 'I did, madam'. The woman looked up, and going back a pace or two, said 'Then I wish you were my husband.'[157]

Carpenter found it easier to relate to the rhythms of Merrill's housekeeping. Charlie Sixsmith says they were both a little fussy together[158] and Carpenter concedes that George got slightly 'houseproud' on occasions but was open to spontaneously abandoning his standards of housework in favour of visits from people he liked.[159] Under the regimes of Mrs Fearnehough and Lucy Adams the sexual division of labour was more clearly marked and spring-cleaning a sacred ritual from which Edward could only flee. With George the domestic work was not divided equally but at least he found it easier to participate. Any notions of commercial gardening were abandoned finally. Now George merely picked flowers and put them in every room and Edward gardened for their needs. He also dusted his study and lit the fire in it every morning.[160]

Edith Lees who, though she married Havelock Ellis, was herself a lesbian and sympathetic to their relationship says it was typical of them to have the piano in the kitchen.

I remember smiling to myself one night when I sat between Carpenter and his factotum and friend in one. One was mending his shirt, and the other a pair of socks. No incongruity struck me, because Carpenter's idea of life is simplification and a real division of work. His belief is, that what a woman can do a man can always share. He has realised the truth that no occupation is a sex monopoly, but a chance for free choice, capability and division of labour. So that when Carpenter takes his share in the washing-up it seems quite as natural as when he lights a cigarette. When he neither sews nor smokes but plays Chopin, a curious realisation comes over one that there is no real difference in the arts of love, music, stocking-mending, or redeeming.[161]

Edward Carpenter did not fully break down the division of labour between classes and between the sexes in his own life. But he did go much further in attempting to distribute the labour in his life democratically than most socialists or anarchists at the time and it really was quite startling for people to observe even this challenge to the order of things. George Merrill's arrival affected more than the housework. He had none of Carpenter's evasive tact and while his frank speaking was extremely handy as a means of getting rid of bores[162] it came as a shock to some of Carpenter's admirers – especially the 'pious or puritanical'[163] whom Merrill loathed. He was careless of what respectable people thought or perhaps simply unconscious of what being 'respectable' meant – either way he did what he wanted.[164] For Edward, painfully self-conscious, seeking an ethical justification for every move, it was delightfully liberatory. Merrill changed the pattern of life somewhat. He liked a drink and visits to the pub became more frequent. He had a repertoire of comic and sentimental popular songs and a good baritone voice. He was familiar with the culture and repartee of the music hall and popular theatres.[165] Merrill brought a very male atmosphere to Millthorpe which was rather bawdy and tended to exclude women.

But Charles Sixsmith felt at home. The Bolton Whitmanites had been meeting since 1885 celebrating Whitman's birthday with songs, speeches, recitations, decorations of lilac boughs and blossoms and much passing of loving cups of comradeship in his memory.[166] After Merrill moved in his visits became more and more frequent and they went on holiday all together to Lyme Regis. He enjoyed Merrill's 'wit' and felt he relieved any dull moments with 'serious minded visitors'.[167] Edith Lees also felt comfortable in the new regime.[168] She liked male company and bawdiness did not offend her. She braved the all-male pub with Carpenter and Merrill and impressed the farm-men by her lack of snobbery and her directness. They were also amazed to meet 'someone more or less resembling a lady'[169] with knowledge of cattle and pig-breeding.

Kate Salt though, possibly because of her own strong feelings towards Edward and her friendship with the Adams, was never reconciled to the relationship between the two men. Again painful estrangement was glossed over in memoirs and autobiographies. But Henry Salt told Alf Mattison that the breach caused by Merrill's arrival never healed and their old intimacy with Carpenter was not restored. 'Kate felt his treatment of *her* very deeply. I was too busy to be greatly troubled; and I had realised years earlier, that Merrill was the evil genius of his life and nothing surprised me.'[170]

If his friends divided over Merrill, the relationship and Merrill's lack of inhibition caused gossip and scandal in the neighbourhood. The country people became more suspicious as the numbers of odd visitors multiplied. Whenever Merrill 'stepped over the line' according to Sixsmith, Carpenter defended him by saying it was his 'childlike spontaneity'.[171] But this did not go down very well with some of the locals. Carpenter claimed that the real country people defended and liked Merrill. It was the 'middling people'[172] who could not get along with him and who spread as scandals his occasional indiscretions.

Despite his devotion to Merrill Carpenter needed to camouflage some aspects of his life. He had written about homosexuality in *Homogenic Love* and later in *Iolaus*. His own homosexuality was no secret within the socialist movement and in the Sheffield area generally. Under the 1885 Act homosexuality was a criminal offence and the Wilde trial in the spring of 1895 contributed towards creating a panic about any discussion of the subject. Carpenter wrote and rewrote *Love's Coming of Age* in order to 'guard against misunderstandings'.[173] He was in double jeopardy as an advocate of the liberation of homosexual love and as a socialist. Underneath his poise he was lonely and he was scared. He may have been aware of some hostility and suspicion from within the left. More directly threatening were attacks from the right. He held off persecution by his vagueness and by the lofty appeals to sentiment in his writing until around 1908 when an Irishman, who lived nearby in Dronfield, began a personal campaign to expose him in the letter column of the *Sheffield Telegraph*. Carpenter had been asked already to debate 'Is Socialism Morally Sound?' in Dronfield Town Hall. He had supporters in the Congregational Church and had evidently already spoken in the church. O'Brien started to follow him to socialist and suffrage meetings. When Carpenter spoke for the Fabians on 'Socialism and State Interference'[174] he challenged him to debate. When Carpenter spoke for the Chesterfield SDF, O'Brien asked him if he meant there would be state interference in introducing young people to vice 'by putting into practice his own infamous teaching on this subject'.[175] Carpenter was an old stager at public speaking and neatly tripped O'Brien up on each occasion and avoided the question but he was nonetheless rattled. Laurence Housman says Carpenter was interrupted during a suffrage meeting and denounced in the 'grossest terms'.[176] He stayed completely calm on the surface and reduced the heckler to insignificance. He was more confident in a large meeting than in more immediate confrontation. Housman says before one meeting of the 'Health Association' Carpenter was very nervous in case O'Brien would be there. 'He would face a crowd of political opponents or a mob of excited jingoes, but he feared the vile slanderer.'[177]

The 'vile slanderer' was busy in February 1909 writing to the *Yorkshire Post* – no more renowned for radicalism than the *Sheffield Telegraph* – declaring that Whitman and his followers formed an 'international revolutionary movement compared with which all other revolutionary movements are mere child's play', and prophesying 'a life and death struggle' which would necessitate heterosexuals taking 'measures of terrible severity' against them.[178] Shortly afterwards he produced a pamphlet attacking Carpenter called *Socialism and Infamy. The Homogenic or Comrade Love Exposed. An Open Letter in Plain Words for a Socialist Prophet to Edward Carpenter.*

It is an extraordinary document. Its author was opposed to Carpenter because he was a socialist, which he felt threatened the family and marriage. But his real horror was of homosexuality. The imagery is vivid, 'putrid cesspool',[179] 'cancer', 'vile Prophets of Sodom and Gomorrah'.[180] Homosexuality is described as a 'disgusting, loathsome, and socially destructive vice'.[181] Arguing for censorship O'Brien asked rhetorically of Carpenter's pamphlet *Homogenic Love*, was it 'calculated to make Sheffield's citizens better husbands, better fathers or better sons ... is it a sound investment for the steel city's sons to invest in? Is it fitted to make mechanics more skilful, intelligent and inventive? Will it increase the industry and efficiency of merchants, organisers, managers, and directors of labour, or of commercial travellers who have to compete for orders in all parts of the civilised world? Is the infamy which is said to have brought destruction upon Sodom and Gomorrah likely to bring in one form or another anything less than destruction upon the trade of Sheffield?'[182]

He was not only concerned about the wealth and morals of the inhabitants of Sheffield, he was personally revolted. 'Embrace and endearment between men ... the very thought of such effeminate practice fills one with loathing.'[183] It would turn men away from their wives to male 'comrades' and make them unfit for 'the duties of the married state'.[184]

O'Brien used all the techniques of the witch-hunt in his accusation of an international conspiracy and his citation of Carpenter's writings. The most immediately threatening aspects of the pamphlet were his attacks on the life of Carpenter and Merrill at Millthorpe. He accused Carpenter of morally poisoning 'thousands of persons of both sexes'[185] who had visited him in his twenty years at Millthorpe, of advocating naked dancing on the hill tops in *Civilisation. Its Cause and Cure*. He even brought Robert Blatchford — a somewhat reluctant sexual radical — into it. Blatchford, by saying no man had a right to himself because he did not make himself, could not logically deny his body 'when some of his dear "comrades" are burning with an ungovernable homogenic love for it'.[186] However, Carpenter's caution and discretion made it difficult to give substance to every specific accusation. O'Brien could only find evidence of Carpenter advocating naked embraces and endearment and quoted a letter from a friend of Carpenter's who had interceded with O'Brien on Carpenter's behalf:

I can assure you from my own observation and knowledge that the particular act which you think Carpenter has in his mind is a very harmless, mild sort of affair. It is the act usually committed by educated and healthy-minded inverts, and consists simply of naked body with naked body in a mutual embrace.[187]

In fact any form of sexual contact between men was illegal and Carpenter was probably protected only by the habitual vagueness of his writing on homosexuality. Even as the anonymous contributor to Havelock Ellis' *Sexual Inversion* he had covered his traces. There appears to have been potentially more direct evidence against George Merrill. O'Brien claimed that there were charges of men being followed and 'molested' which had not been 'pressed home simply because those who make them do not like their names to be mixed up with anything that is so vile and loathsome'.[188]

O'Brien did not just publish his pamphlet. He appeared in

Holmesfield with a satchel full and left one at the Hukins', handing it to Fannie at the door.[189] He was hoping that carpenter would sue him for libel.[190] George Hukin said he seemed to be mad but that he would be dangerous. As long as he just based his accusations on Carpenter's writings he would do little.[191] But there were some nasty rumours and embarrassment in the village and George Merrill appears to have been the real source of scandal.

Hukin said the schoolmaster, the parish council and the vicar were all indignant. It was a kind of guilt by association as they had by this time known Carpenter for many years and he had eventually become a councillor. The vicar said he had no reason to believe Carpenter had 'lived anything but an absolutely clear life'.[192] Hukin's old experience of backroom politics suddenly came to the fore in the crisis. He had worked out what everyone's reaction was, calculating where there was danger and where it was safe. Hukin estimated that they were left most exposed by George Merrill's devil-may-care behaviour:

'G' [sic] is the real problem with all the stories going about concerning him. I think it would be wise to keep him away for the present. Of course one does not know how much O'Brien knows still one must be careful at present. Strange stories are afloat. Fannie told me yesterday that two different women had told her that a number of women at Dronfield were anxious to know when you were returning that they might waylay and mob you. I don't set much store by these tales although I daresay O'Brien has managed to stir up a good deal of feeling against you in that particular quarter.[193]

O'Brien continued his attacks later in 1909 and in 1910 when elections came up Carpenter's name was at the bottom of the poll. They had to lose a councillor so he was dropped.[194] It was all done very tactfully but O'Brien had had some effect. The laboriously created world of Millthorpe and friends was vulnerable. There was a moment of real peril. Despite the protection of a private income and his gentleman's breeding Carpenter's freedom was fragile. However, the whole affair passed over. O'Brien was imprisoned for some offence and after that he was never seen again in the area.

### Carpenter's Relationships with Women

The imagined antagonism of the village women is an indication of the effect on women of the close bonds between the men in Carpenter's circle at Millthorpe. The responses of working-class women directly affected by the relations of their men-folk were never recorded. The women never emerge in the correspondence from their shadowy status as wives. They exist in a twilight women's world of mysterious ailments, unaccountable depressions, patterns of visiting, spring cleaning and recipes. For instance Fannie Hukin suffered with neuralgia in the winter of 1890 when George Hukin was groaning about Robert Bingham's speech in court.[195] It was apparently a recurring complaint as Hukin was still referring to her neuralgia a year later, saying it was better.[196] In the autumn of 1891 he was rarely at home because of his efforts to organise the razor-grinders. There were meetings five nights a week and Fannie is described – not surprisingly – as 'out of sorts'.[197] There *was* a lighter side to life. In the days of their courtship there were precious walks and evenings alone together. When they were first married and still deeply involved in the socialist club there were the social evenings, the tea and cards with Lucy and George Adams.[198] Later the odd outing is mentioned. Fannie and George Hukin visited London for example in January 1893,[199] there were holidays in Morecambe from the mid-nineties. Then the rise of the Independent Labour Party and the Labour Church meant there was still the occasional 'do' where they could meet old friends even though they were not as committed as they had been in the 1880s. In March 1895 for example, Fannie Hukin, George Hukin, George Adams, Lucy Adams, George Merrill, and 'Annie I' – possibly Annie Fearnehough – were all at an Independent Labour Party dance in Sheffield.[200]

It is not clear whether Fannie Hukin knew of her husband's relationship with Carpenter but Mrs Fearnehough and Lucy Adams must have been aware of his homosexuality because they lived at Millthorpe. Mrs Fearnehough is an almost non-existent character in Carpenter's correspondence. He remembers her absent-mindedly when he writes to Kate Salt with some new recipes which might cheer her up.[201] She spring-cleans for him in the midst of anarchist trials: 'My room has come out a fiery red.'[202] Mrs Fearnehough appears to have been friendly with Furniss' wife – an even more remote figure – and Lucy Adams seems to have been quite close to Fanny Hukin.[203] But it is unfortunately impossible to know what the women talked about among themselves or to discover how they countered the intensity of the connection between the men. Events of considerable importance to the women are glanced over in the men's letters, childbirth, the upbringing of the children, for example, are rarely mentioned at all. Though George Hukin did find time to tell Carpenter in November 1891 that Lucy Adams was in bed with a 'miscarriage or something of that sort. Anyway the threatened addition to the family is averted.'[204] It is evident that if the world of the women had been documented as extensively as the world of the men a quite different picture of life at Millthorpe would emerge.

It must have been a big change for Mrs Fearnehough when she left the security of Millthorpe and strange too for Lucy Adams to adjust to living in the countryside. When the Adams first took the Fearnehoughs' place Lucy Adams evidently found it difficult to settle.[205] The housework must have presented problems too. There was Carpenter's idiosyncratic routine and diet. Apart from his extraordinary visitors, there were young ladies, slightly odd, but still young ladies, Kate Salt, Olive Schreiner, Kate Conway, Isabella Ford and Carpenter's sisters and even a 'worldly cousin' in 1894.[206] They must have all made rather different demands on Lucy Adams, regarding her sometimes as a servant. Thus while the advanced women like Olive Schreiner would write to her as a friend[207] the 'worldly cousin' and possibly even the sisters must have expected her to keep her place in a more conventional way.

In immediate practical terms the household labour which does not appear to have been shared in the Fearnehoughs' and Adams' regimes must have become arduous despite all the simplification. At first Mrs Fearnehough was helped by her daughter Annie, and when Annie left to work in Sheffield she missed her, 'especially on washing days'.[208] Washing for all the inhabitants and guests must have been an exhausting task in those days, when everything had to be done by hand and each operation required more hot water. Similarly shopping for a variable number of people even with the help of produce from the garden would be a complicated task. After the Fearnehoughs had left Carpenter described 'struggles in Dronfield and other places to get provisions' to Kate Salt in 1894.[209]

He was certainly more aware than most of his contemporaries of the nature of working women's labour in the home. Simply because his politics were explicitly committed to revealing the connection between personal life and political activity there was at least a possibility of reflecting on the women's inner world. But we are still left with reflections. The women's material circumstances, the nature of the everyday life which formed their vision of the world, remain obscure. The sexual division of labour remained, so they played a secondary part in the formal politics of the club. They were also excluded from the circle of male comradeship. There is a point beyond which Carpenter does not probe the boundaries of his class and sex. The new life never reached the working-class women round the Sheffield socialist club as strongly as it did the men. The concern with the richness of the heart, with personal relations, the struggle to be open despite class differences, faltered in relation to working-class women. This failure, almost a bored negligence, confined the radical implications of Carpenter's politics in practice to the working men in his circle. The sexual feelings which brought them together also created a defensiveness against the women, which it must have been hard for them not to resent. Given the prevailing personal relationships between the classes and between the sexes it is difficult to see how it could have been otherwise. Nonetheless the extent to which Carpenter and his friends could present a challenge to domestic relationships was reduced because its intensity was limited to one sex.

Just as there was a crucial blurring in the actual class

inequalities between the men, the real differences between the role of working-class men and women in the circle were never confronted and acknowledged. This in turn affected the way in which working-class women were pictured by the men and ultimately how all women were seen. Carpenter could deal with working-class women he could idealise as maternal figures. Louisa Usher is portrayed cosily 'large-bosomed and large hearted'.[210] Mrs Maloy − perhaps less cosy − is hardly mentioned in Carpenter's writing, nor are the younger women in the socialist club, Lucy Adams and Fannie Hukin, described in any detail. Older working-class women were distanced and became the objects of generalised admiration and philosophy. For example, when Alf Mattison's mother died he remembered the welcome she gave him twenty-five years before in Hunslet with 'What endless patience and devotion these mothers exhibit. From what deep source in the universal life do they draw it.'[211]

Marching down Kirkstall Road in Leeds with Alf Mattison and the ILP on a May Day in the 1890s with strains of *England Arise* coming from the marchers, Carpenter eyed the 'crowds of working-class women with babes at their breasts and at their feet' and turned to Alf saying 'Ah these populations. The faces of these poor women look so tragic.'[212] Describing the mother of his lover George Merrill, he picked out her physical enormity and 'raciness'.[213] There was always a romantic gloss to his realism.

Working-class women remained symbols of an ideal of motherhood, nurture, suffering, labour, strength and earthiness. Carpenter, though involved in intense relations with women of his own class as well as with working-class men, was unable to overcome the divisions of class and sex together. As for the working-class men in the inner ring, George Hukin's affection for Fannie is evident and both he and George Adams shared their political lives with Fannie and Lucy to some extent at least. But Hukin's friendship with Carpenter must have meant some exclusion of Fannie. Jim Shortland's family life was less happy for he left his wife and children and went into lodgings in 1901.[214] George Merrill appears to have been emotionally intimate with young working-class women although never sexually attracted to them. According to Carpenter he would talk freely with them about 'a hundred little things which men do not generally appreciate'. When he was living at Millthorpe 'the girls and young married women were constantly telling him all sorts of things about themselves – about their love affairs, and coming babies and so forth and I believe that he really helped them a good deal with his quaint experience and advice'.[215] Merrill's openness could cross the sex division though his relations with upper-class women were more uneasy. Alf Mattison was probably the most comfortable in women's company. He had a long and continuing friendship with Isabella and Bessie Ford. He knew and liked Olive Schreiner with whom he was at Millthorpe in the summer of 1893.[216] Florence Mattison, the woman he married, is the only working-class woman among Carpenter's close circle who seems to have been herself deeply involved in politics. She was active in the Leeds feminist and socialist movements, sharing her husband's affection and admiration for Olive Schreiner.[217]

Carpenter undoubtedly found relationships with his middle-class women friends much easier. There was quite a circle of them which included Helena Born, Miriam Daniell, Katherine Glasier from Bristol, Isabella Ford from Leeds, Olive Schreiner, Edith Lees and of course Kate Salt. They have left their testimony of friendship in letters and memoirs. There was disagreement about how understanding Carpenter was of women. Henry Salt maintained Schreiner and Ford believed he did not really comprehend much.[218] Edith Lees on the other hand thought he had special insights. Younger women who did not know him personally appear to have found him approachable as a kind of spiritual adviser. Perhaps his homosexuality gave him a detachment from masculinity which women found sympathetic. Because of his life and his writing he became something of a cult figure which must have been frightening for him.[219] Young lady Fabians marched determinedly to visit Millthorpe in the rain. When Hyndman's cousin began seeing visions of a person by her bedside who she declared was Edward Carpenter, Carpenter wrote ironically to Alf

Mattison, 'It may be so but I know nothing of visiting the bedrooms of ladies at midnight.'[220]

Much more serious was Carpenter's entanglement with Kate Salt. Like Edith Lees and Olive Schreiner she read and commented on his writings about sexual liberation. He depended on her and was grateful for her criticisms. They were happy playing their duets together. He confided his everyday problems to her. But from his first gift of Olive Schreiner's *Story of an African Farm* in 1889[221] it was evident that he could never feel for her as she felt for him and no gifts could compensate for this. The inequality in the relationship humiliated her. She became over-conscious of her effect on him and unable to be herself. This made him irritable when they were together. So she clung on to memories of happy moments: 'I feed on kind looks and words. I feel nearer to you when we are away than when you are near.'[222]

It was possible for her to dwell on their spiritual communion and ignore any physical incompatibility until Merrill with his intense male sexuality negated this fragile love. The year before George Merrill and Edward Carpenter were able to live together Kate Salt's longing erupted in panic and desperation:

Edward – don't leave me altogether if you can help it. I have really tried hard and sometimes I feel as if I shall go down but when I feel I am absolutely nothing to you it seems impossible to go on. After all why should I pretend and dissemble? It can't do any good. Forgive me and don't refuse me utterly (inwardly I mean) remember that all this time it has been blank, black darkness to me and there's something in me that denies it all the time, denies that you can want to cut and lop me off altogether . . . Edward I want your hand still.[223]

In a few months she had become calmer. Their friendship survived but in a different way.

Kate Salt worked as Bernard Shaw's secretary for a time and his observation on the triangular relationship between the Salts and Carpenter is characteristically uncharitable. After Shaw's marriage in 1898, his wife pressurised him to break with Carpenter and sexual unorthodoxies – in his old age Shaw was particularly inclined to jibe at the doings of his early friends. He called Kate Salt a 'hybrid' and a 'homo' and commented,

Salt's tragedy was that his wife . . . would not consummate their marriage calling herself an Urning. She got it from her close friend Edward Carpenter who taught Kate that Urnings are a chosen race.

Shaw says that he and Carpenter were 'Sunday husbands' to her and that Henry Salt was quite 'in the friendship'. They were bound by a Shelleyan friendship which denied exclusive love. Perhaps Bernard Shaw's masculine pride was touched for he was irritated by Kate Salt's refusal of her husband and declares 'she was always falling in love with some woman'.[224]

Whatever the truth of Kate Salt's sexual emotions she suffered along with the other free women in the circle from the difficulty of expressing emotion without being engulfed by it. She believed so strongly in the liberation of women yet in her own life idealised Carpenter and Shaw. She submerged her own considerable abilities in caring for her husband and giving support and encouragement to men like Carpenter.

Even among the middle-class circle the general relationships between the men have a certain primacy. If it was difficult for male homosexual love to escape from the underworld of brothel and sexual exploitation and assert its own validity, the women had really greater difficulties. Lesbianism remains somehow by the way, implicit and inarticulate. It was probably more emotional then openly sexual. In the late Victorian context feeling was much more acceptable between women than between men. Apart from Edith Lees' lesbianism, there are hints here and there, in Born and Daniel's unconventional closeness, and in Shaw's description of Kate Salt. But a conscious identification with a lesbian role seems to belong to a later period, emerging just after the First World War. Carpenter in his writing on *The Intermediate Sex* speaks very much for men.

This is more generally true also of his writing on sexuality for however much he might feel that he could transcend class and sex divisions in his personal life, he remained still an upper-middle-class man. Although he was exceptionally perceptive and committed to living his beliefs he could not escape the consequences of his actual position in the world. His thinking began from this situation which was one of sympathetic privilege. The extraordinary record he has left us of the inner relationships within the socialist movement becomes blurred where his perception faltered at the class and sex divide. Consequently we have no means of knowing what working-class women in his circle thought and felt. For all his closeness of observation he wrote about women's oppression from outside. He could listen to his friends like Kate Salt, Edith Lees and Olive Schreiner but perhaps not to Lucy Adams and Fannie Hukin.

So, not surprisingly, it is his own predicament as a middle-class man which is thrown into relief by the ambiguities of his relationship to women. He writes with respect about the changing consciousness of women but his real passion is reserved for the emotional distortion he had experienced in being a man. He writes of the tearing pain of class estrangement and the upper-class reserve which wrenches out warmth. He knew how the denial of sexual feeling closed up the heart and he knew the loneliness of belonging nowhere. Hence the longing for community and comradeship. His socialism protested against the inevitability of the grotesque inner break he bore along with other men of his class and background. Carpenter's homosexuality undoubtedly awakened his awareness of this split between what was socially expected of men, and the real force of his own desires. But it was not only a homosexual situation, it was more generally the predicament of masculinity. The price of sex privilege among men of his class was the denial of feeling between men. The expression of feeling suggested exposure, vulnerability, passivity, dependence and terror. It indicated that a man of the ruling class was not all he was supposed to be. Carpenter, with his sandals, his cottage and his conscience quietly following the heart and suggesting that others might do so to advantage struck at the delicate division of emotional labour which helped to keep class and sex domination in its place.

**Books and Ideas**

In his reply to the congratulatory letter from his friends on his seventieth birthday Edward Carpenter claimed no credit as a reformer. 'After all, what a man does he does out of necessity of his nature.' He thought it was a

good general rule . . . that people should endeavour (more than they do) to express or liberate their own real and deep-rooted needs and feelings. Then in doing so they will probably liberate and aid the expression of the lives of thousands of others, and so will have the pleasure of helping, without the unpleasant sense of laying anyone under an obligation.[225]

Throughout all his writings there is a belief which he shared with the romantics in a 'real' human nature. The search is to restore this nature, to achieve a new unity between the inner self and the outer world which would allow a rebirth of the human spirit. In *Towards Democracy* (1881–82) the realisation of this liberation is expressed as a dual relationship with our own bodies and with other people. Recognising our physical needs is a basic means of centring ourselves. The body he says 'is a root of the soul'.[226] It is the means by which humanity can return to the dark earth, the old goat-footed god of desire:

Sex still goes first, and hands, eyes, mouth, brain follow; from the midst of belly and thighs radiate the knowledge of self, religion and immortality.[227]

This shameless, wild, lusty, unpresentable creature is the means of rebirth – 'of the despised one hobbling on hoofs – I dream'. Through union with 'the despised one', with democracy, the individual self becomes level with the poor, the prostitute, the criminal, the mad people and so fuses with all humanity. This is not an external but a personal relation. But before those 'burdened of everyday . . . the over-worked and hope-forlorn'[228] can be released there is the external apparatus of government and power which holds them to be overcome. Carpenter's non-exclusive mysticism necessitates social engagement. In *Towards Democracy* he expresses all the hatred and revulsion which had been gathering in him about the behaviour and attitudes of his own class. He presents the upper classes living in 'careful obedience' in the 'prison life of custom without one touch of nature',[229] consumed with false values. They have no real relationship to the making of things, to materials and no connection to their own inner selves. They are cut off from one another as they are from themselves:

When the surface-test is final . . . a trick of clothing or speech, metallic clink in the pocket, white skin, soft hands, fawning and lying looks – everywhere the thrust of rejection, the bond of redemption nowhere.[230]

The false relations of the upper class permeate the whole of society distorting all human relationships,

that men disbelieve in the human heart and think that the source of power is set otherwhere than in its burning glowing depths, that the powers which they worship are but so many withered emblems of power – dead scoriae nodding and jostling over the living lava-stream.[231]

There were the scoriae which had reclaimed his friend Andrew Beck, punished Jane Olivia Daubeny, crushed his mother and which threatened to contain him. Between 1883 and 1886 he declared a kind of war on them by his life, his politics, and his intellectual work. He started speaking for socialist groups and his talks were printed first as articles and then as *England's Ideal* (1884), *Simplification of Life, Private Property, The Enchanted Thicket* (1886). He repeated his attacks on the falsity of conventional upper-class life and the distortion in human relationships which the class system created. In *Civilisation: Its Cause and Cure* (1889), he challenged the complacency which saw civilisation as the height of progress. On the contrary, he said, civilisation was a 'disease'. Disease for him implied a loss of unity, a split. He followed the evolutionary anthropologist Lewis Morgan, who was also to influence Engels' *Origin of the Family*, in believing that the institution of private property and the growth of a class system was responsible for this separation. Within nineteenth-century anthropology there was a current of thought which believed in a lost Golden Age of primitive communism. It was thought that myths and legends could be used as historical evidence to prove the existence of this era. Not only did he think such a society had existed but Carpenter believed that, in a sense, it was still there. This health, sense of wholeness, holiness was carried in everyone, 'each human soul . . . bears within itself some kind of reminiscence of a more harmonious soul'.[232]

He thought the people who had been by-passed by civilisation were nearest to this unity. He looked not only to the working class and to women but to the outcast, the outlaws, criminals. As a homosexual he could go out towards the despised and neglected. Carpenter was also inclined to stress the oppressive nature of 'civilisation', of all industrial society not just capitalism. His politics carried elements of utopian socialism and anarchism in their yearning for a lost harmony and their emphasis on subjective transformation. While it had been Hyndman's *England for All* which had crystallised his socialism, he regarded the SDF leader himself as like a 'shop whose goods are all in the front window'.[233] The contemporary marxism of the SDF which Carpenter knew emphasised change in the external fabric of society. For Hyndman the inevitable crisis was just round the corner. Carpenter, who had rejected secularism because it saw the universe as a mechanism, was too preoccupied with inner consciousness to accept a version of marxism which denied interaction between the individual and external social reality. He had, like Morris, a more total vision of the transformation of all social relations. He was consistently suspicious of a socialism which required only changes in the ownership of production, the substitution of the state for the employer, the centralisation of government or labour representation in parliament. Consequently he was not happy with the SDF's marxism, with the Fabians or with labourism. He inclined towards Kropotkin's anarchism with its emphasis on decentralisation, mutual aid and lack of government but recoiled from the anarchism of Nicoll and Creaghe and its immersion in violent propaganda by deed. After the collapse of the Socialist League Carpenter became in practice close to the Independent Labour Party. But this connection which persisted into the 1900s was based on local contact not on the leadership in London and he was always ready to speak for other groups, Fabians, SDF or the labour churches. In the 1890s and 1900s his talks could draw large numbers. He could attract as many as two thousand people to a meeting at the Labour Church or Sheffield Hall of Science. In Yorkshire, Lancashire, and the Midlands he continued to be a well-known figure. His early links with Bristol and Glasgow survived.[234]

He spoke in a network of clubs and institutions in the 1900s which had been formed in the late nineteenth century. Edward Carpenter was at home in this local socialist culture which continued to have its own life regardless of party divisions at the centre of organisations.

In 1909–10 some of these local groupings were evidently interested in what he called 'The Larger Socialism' – this was socialism expanded to include his ideas of non-parasitic living, simplification of life, the liberation of women and respect for animals. He gave this lecture to Meesbrook ILP in October 1909, and to Manchester ILP in November of the same year. In February 1910 he was speaking at Stockport Labour Church and for the Fabians in Liverpool and Chesterfield in March, then for Blackburn ILP in October and the Clarion club in Glasgow in November 1910.[235] 'The Larger Socialism' transcended all denominations.

In the changed context of the 1900s Edward Carpenter became estranged from old friends like Bruce Glasier who had become preoccupied with the beginnings of a labour parliamentary machine. His political sympathies went towards new movements at odds with this parliamentary labourism. The militancy of the syndicalists and the suffragettes awakened memories of the 1880s more than parliamentary manœuvring. He was excited by Victor Grayson's victory in the Colne Valley by-election as an independent revolutionary socialist in 1907. Grayson's moral enthusiasm, his refusal to reduce socialism to immediate tactical priorities echoed the hopes of the '80s. Guild Socialism, with its dismissal of politics, its concern to moralise the organisation of production was also attractive and he supported the journal *The New Age* edited by his friend A.R.Orage which argued for Guild Socialism.

Carpenter found a dialectical philosophical basis for his politics in the mild Hegelian idealism which influenced English thinkers in the late nineteenth century. He shared their stress on personal action and the longing for harmony and unity, their desire to transcend the world as it was with the world as they thought it should be, in order to evade the resolution of contradiction by conflict. The effort to avoid conflict tended to lead to a denial of the existence of the real world. Philosophically Carpenter never accepted this extreme idealism which denied that matter existed. Instead he thought matter gained meaning only when it had consciousness projected upon it.[236] Similarly in his politics he recognised the constraint of external social reality. For example, he was not attracted by the Sheffield anarchist-communists' extreme voluntarism which saw revolution as an act of will. More generally his mysticism did not go inwards and become restricted to an elite. It was outgoing and all embracing. He wanted to transform social relationships and release the potential of all humanity. He was a democratic mystic. This did not mean of course that he was able always to balance the inner and outer reality. The very intensity of his preoccupation with the inner self often made him lose touch with the outer world. The dialectic becomes an internal system.

Science became a substitute materialism and was the other side of this idealism. Biological analogies of social change were popular in the period. Darwin's theory of evolution was used as a model for society. Survival of the fittest in a competitive environment became a popular justification for class and racial domination in capitalism. This environmental determinism influenced not only the right-wing social Darwinists, but also some of the socialists from the Fabians through to the SDF. In opposition Carpenter presented his theories of 'exfoliation'. The term was borrowed from Whitman and expressed the shedding of old forms and the growth of the new within the shell of the old. Despite his own suspicions he was still within this contemporary idiom of thought in producing 'scientific' justification. He favoured Lamarck's theories of evolution because they allowed more scope for inner growth than external accident. Here he was close to the anarchists. Kropotkin's *Mutual Aid* argued a similar case.

A persistent theme in his writing is the existence of some kind of consciousness beyond reason, some older knowingness carried within all of us, a common natural humanity outside history. There were several sources for this belief. Initially it came from his love of the romantics especially Shelley, then from Walt Whitman. It was reinforced by his interest in Eastern religious thought. A Canadian friend of Carpenter's, Dr Bucke, described this knowingness as 'Cosmic Consciousness'.[237]

In the 1900s Carpenter's own thinking coincided with a more general intellectual rejection of nineteenth-century mechanical determinism and liberal rationalism. Philosophical ideas of an inner creative vitalism and a desire to explore the irrational combined in artistic movements and in the growth of psychoanalysis. Carpenter's writing thus assumed a brief relevance before it was overtaken by the twentieth century. Subjectivism, vitalism, cosmic consciousness, the irrational, the primitive, art, magic and nature were to be appropriated in the 1920s and '30s by people who felt they were outside all political systems of thought or by the new fascist right. But in the last years of the nineteenth century and in the 1900s this division was less clear. It was still possible to be a socialist and search for the dark gods and for rebirth through a unity of inner soul with the outer world without being seen as an eccentric. Carpenter's writing in the 1890s and 1900s could thus feed into a cultural and political rejection of nineteenth-century capitalism and the dominant ideology of liberal rationalism which influenced a new generation of socialists.

There were, however, aspects of his thought which were less in tune with the common assumptions of contemporary socialism. His interest in Indian mysticism and his commitment to sexual liberation – homosexual as well as heterosexual – was difficult to assimilate even for this eclectic socialist culture. His fascination for the East came partly from his struggle against a mechanistic universe. It had also personal sources. His elder brother went to work in India. He had a college friend, P. Arunáchalam, who taught him how to make the sandals he loved to wear along the Derbyshire lanes and which he sent to friends all over the world, believing in the freedom of feet from boots. The fascination was also partly political – the radical Englishman's rejection of his imperial heritage. Harold Cox, an English college friend, was in Northern India from the mid-1880s and sent Carpenter news of the nationalist aspirations of the Indian people.[238] Unlike Cox and many of his political associates Carpenter's anti-imperialism held firm in the 1890s. At the time of the Boer War he wrote 'Empire' in which he described two Englands, one a withered and hollow tree with the 'yellow dirt'[239] of imperial domination, the other a seedling, a possibility of new democratic growth.

He realised that Indian nationalism would become a power-ful force which must end the British hold over India. The external bond of Empire would dissolve. Characteristically though, he hoped for some inner union between the two races.

This hope of personal communication could only be achieved through equal cultural exchange, not through the brash assumption of western superiority. Carpenter did not surrender himself com-pletely, remaining uneasy about the political consequences of the passivity of Eastern religious faith and impatient with sham crazes for Mahatmas.[240] But his interest first in the *Bhagavad-Gita* and then in Hinduism confirmed by his visit to India and Ceylon in 1890 exercised an important influence on his ideas.

In an Indian Gnani he found another Whitman and in Hindu thought he found a way of developing the feelings expressed in *Towards Democracy*. He could see a means of attaining the consciousness without thought, and beyond words, which he felt existed alongside the self-consciousness which was expressed in western rationalism.[241] By touching this consciousness humanity could transcend the 'crack' between mind and nature. The realisation of the individual self was not as in Christianity through denial but through merging with the universe. God was within you.[242]

He describes his travels and experiences in *From Adam's Peak to Elephanta*. He told how he had visited the Gnani and clambered through the forests and how while climbing Adam's Peak he came to see his guide as a kind of Caliban. Carpenter lived in the open on bananas and coconuts on this nature pilgrimage and watched an erotic 'Night Festival in a Hindu temple'.

It was an unconventional passage to India for an English member of the upper classes and his book upset the British establishment in India. The reviews were icy both about his support for Indian nationalism and his enthusiasm for Indian culture. *The Athenaeum* was particularly testy about his discovery of a secret English nudist colony in Bombay called 'The Fellowship of the Naked Trust' who made Carpenter an honorary member and had a district sessions judge as president. *The Athenaeum* apparently thought that imperialists without clothes might lose their authority.[243]

His talks and writings on sexual relationships date from his return from India, his meeting with George Merrill and the change in political organisation marked by the collapse of the Socialist League and the emergence of the Independent Labour Party. His talks appeared in pamphlets from 1894 and were grouped together as *Love's Coming of Age* in 1896. The Wilde trial in 1895 made his publishers Fisher Unwin afraid to include his writing on homosexuality and this section was not inserted until 1906.

In *Love's Coming of Age* Carpenter traced the origin of women's oppression from the introduction of private property. The influence of Morgan, Olive Schreiner and the German socialist Bebel are evident. He described the differing predicaments of the 'lady', the household drudge and the prostitute in the late nineteenth century. He believed that only communism could free women because only a non-competitive society could support women when they were mothers without depending on a man. He writes of how the women of his day were prevented from expressing their feelings, crushed by household labour or treated as sexual property. His best writings are his observant, carefully detailed sketches of oppression which came from his life in Brighton and Sheffield.

He also tried to understand how men were affected by oppressing women. Again his experience with men of his own class is very evident. Man is presented as the 'Ungrown'. There he is a boy at public school 'well pounded into shape, kneaded and baked', for the 'upper crust'. Gliding into a career he settles into 'beefy self-satisfaction'. There is no space for the development of 'affection and tenderness of feeling':[244]

A man pelts along on his hobby – his business, his career, his latest invention, or what not – forgetful that there is such a thing in the world as the human heart; then all of a sudden he 'falls in love', tumbles headlong in the most ludicrous way, fills the air with his cries, struggles frantically like a fly in treacle: and all the time hasn't the faintest idea whether he has been inveigled into the situation, or whether he got there of his own accord, or what he wants now he is there.[245]

The consequences of this emotional neglect were serious for these unbaked creatures, these 'nincompoops',[246] who held the lives of others in their power. In opposition to them Carpenter hails the rebellion of women and he calls on women to declare themselves free women:

Let every woman whose heart bleeds for the sufferings of her sex, hasten to declare herself and to constitute herself as far as she possibly can, a free woman. Let her accept the term with all the odium that belongs to it; let her insist on her right to speak, dress, think, act and above all to use her sex, as she deems best; let her face the scorn and the ridicule; let her 'loose her own life' if she likes; assured that only so can come deliverance, and that only when the free woman is honoured will the prostitute cease to exist. And let every man who really would respect his counter-part, entreat her also to act so; let him never by word or deed tempt her to grant as a bargain what can only be precious as a gift; let him see her with pleasure stand a little aloof; let him help her to gain her feet.[247]

It was characteristic of the emphasis in his politics on consciousness that he calls for this liberation by cultural declaration. There is no understanding of how to reach this liberation so the space is filled by exhortation to heroic defiance.

This limitation though was an important feature of the contemporary socialist and anarchist movements' general approach. Women's liberation was not regarded as a necessity coming from the contradictory movement of capitalist society. It was still seen as an ethical question which socialists *ought* to support. The relationship of personal cultural change to the total system of capitalist oppression remained implicit. So for Carpenter, along with other socialists and anarchists who wanted to assert sexual liberation, the understanding of what was wrong was divorced from any clear ideal of what could be done. Nora slamming the door of the *Doll's House* was the symbolic declaration of the new woman's revolt. But what could women do who were not as strong as Nora and who were too bound by social circumstance to fight alone? In the 1900s the existence of a feminist movement shifted the discussion somewhat so the idea of women gaining strength through collective action was possible. But neither socialists nor feminists were able to develop a theory which could fully explain the specific oppression of women and its relationship to the exploitation of the worker in capitalism.

Carpenter's *Love's Coming of Age* nonetheless made some significant innovation within the terms of contemporary discussion of sexual politics.

In his book he does not deny the complexity of sexual desire. He tried to probe the irrational and come to terms with deep sexual passion. He added for example a note 'On Jealousy' in which he tried to distinguish between initial preoccupation with a lover's uniqueness and artificial property jealousy which he thought was 'the product of immediate social conditions'.[248] Carpenter also grasped the significance of the separation of sexual pleasure from procreation, though he was initially suspicious of contraceptives because he thought they were designed for the man's satisfaction at the expense of the woman's.

His acceptance of the range and variety of human sexual feeling, his willingness to accept the irrational and contradictory came from his own sexual predicament, and from the studies of early sex psychologists like Ellis. He was in contact with sexual radicals in Germany who were discussing all aspects of human sexuality, seeking a science of sexual relations.

There is too the American tradition of sexual utopianism with its origins in the communities where perfectionists sought not only a new relationship to labour but to the body. Sexual pleasure was part of this perfectionism. Contraceptives were sometimes suspect as artificial and mechanical aids. This tradition favoured internal control. For instance John Humphrey Noyes at the Oneida community devised a system of 'male continence' which appears to have been the diversion of semen into the urinary tract.[249]

Carpenter's publisher in America, Alice B. Stockham, advocated prolonged intercourse without emission in *Karezza*.[250] This approach to sexuality which related to Carpenter's interest in Eastern eroticism emphasised an exchange of power. The aim was union through conscious control rather than the orgasm as achievement of genital release.

Edward Carpenter's writing was thus important in popularising the development of German sex psychology and in carrying the radical utopian insistence on the significance of sexual pleasure and control over the body to British socialists.

Nonetheless he followed other contemporary socialist writers like Engels in assuming that the sexual division of labour was natural because of the biological difference between men and women and he accepted 'masculinity' and 'feminity' as fixed characteristics. This had important effects on his theories not only about heterosexual relationships but about homosexuality. It is a continuing theme from his first pamphlet in 1894 published by the Manchester Labour Press *Homogenic Love and its Place in a Free Society* through *The Intermediate Sex* (1908) to *Intermediate Types amongst Primitive Folk* in 1914. Indeed by 1914 he was using a species of eugenic argument popular at the time to argue that the combination of male and female characteristics which he found in his intermediate types was an indication of their superiority. He was concerned to justify homosexuality by producing examples of exceptionally talented homosexuals.[251]

In his *Days with Walt Whitman* published in 1906 there is a hint of the homosexual love as transcending sex divisions. This was clearly stated in 1922 in a talk on Whitman for the British Society for the Study of Sex Psychology:

if ever there is to be evolved a higher type of humanity of such a nature as to include male and female characteristics, it is pretty certain that on the way to that ideal will occur lop-sided and unbalanced types straying far in one or the other direction, but that we need not on that account abandon our faith in an ultimate and admirable result. . . . After all the continuation of the race is not the main object of love and sex intercourse . . . the main thing is the actual establishment of and consolidation of a new form of life – the double life.[252]

The evolution of acquired characteristics is assumed, there is an internal process developing towards an ideal. The ideal transcends actual divisions between men and women who are described as possessing fixed gender characteristics. He did not pursue the radical implications of separating sexuality and procreation as a political question which related to people's actual lives. Instead it remains as an ideal androgyny, a 'new form of life – the double life'. The disassociation of sex from procreation was essential both for the free expression of homosexual love and for the feminist demand of birth control. But Carpenter does not struggle to free sexuality from the tyranny of gender.

An androgynous stereotype ignores how all our notions of what a man is and what a woman is are created by the totality of our social relationships and by the circumstances of our own sexual practice. These notions express the past and the moment now. They are changing both with the movement of society and with our own sexual political doings. Carpenter obscures this with the ideal of androgyny – a projection of now into the future which hardens into a stereotype – an external structure to be lived up to as 'a higher type of humanity'.[253]

Carpenter was critical of the social association of feminity with inferiority. He carefully adds that the love of women for one another should be included within this sexual 'evolution'. But lesbian love is overwhelmed by his real passion which is for a male comradeship. The democratic vision of affective sexuality extending itself through the world becomes narrowed to an *elite*, a superior brotherhood.

Even within his own terms Carpenter's notions of transcendent androgyny remained remarkably sex-bound. It was all very well for men to carry fixed feminine characteristics and gain a power to see through the divide between the sexes. But it appears to go wrong when it is applied to women in practice. In *Love's Coming of Age* Carpenter stereotypes feminists in ways that are indistinguishable from heterosexual male fantasies of commanding women. Some of the feminists he says are women without strong sexual or maternal instincts. Some are 'mannish' in temperament; some are 'homogenic', that is, inclined to attachments to their own, rather than to the opposite sex; some are ultra-rationalising and 'brain-cultured'.[254]

The other aspect of this is his depiction of working-class women as symbols of motherhood and labour rather like the peasant women in Millet's paintings which he greatly admired. Women as individuals acting in particular social situations are lost on these stereotypes. A universal 'woman' replaces real women either as the ideal 'free woman' or as the caricatured 'men' or he reduces her to the biological role of reproducer. This is the equivalent of the idealisation of the manual worker as the personification of the dignity of labour.

His idealism, his scientific analogies for social change, and his confusion of sex and gender all carried an implicit conservatism which constrained the radical influence of his sexual theory and meant it could be absorbed within liberal apologies for homosexuality. However, he lived and worked in the context of a determinist form of marxism, of eugenic assumptions in which a wide range of acquired characteristics like drunkenness and criminality were still being seen as biologically inherited. Carpenter attempted to assert a dialectic between personal sexual life and the institutions of society in the effort to understand the relationship of subjective consciousness and external social relations, with inadequate theoretical equipment. He was aware how inadequate were explanations of human consciousness which saw large historical forces alone as responsible for all our perceptions. Since he wrote, these questions have been steered off into specific debates within aesthetics or psychoanalysis. But the emergence of the women's and gay movements and of anti-psychiatry have raised them again as part of radical politics. Carpenter, the sexual theorist, would have understood the controversies within these movements, just as we can find his writing still of interest. His insistence in the 1890s and early 1900s that society had exaggerated the differences between the sexes and that there was a possibility of changing the sexual division of labour, not only by women doing men's work but by men helping with household labours, was extremely radical. So too was his faith in human sexual experience indicating the possibility of a much fuller physical and mental realisation if the inner and outer bondages could be dissolved.

### Connections

Carpenter's life and ideas raise wider questions about the socialist movement in the late nineteenth and early twentieth centuries which have still to be explored. This is partly because of his importance outside London. We still know organisations from the centre. But even local studies of a socialist grouping can miss many aspects of the personal experience of its members unless we ask consciously how did these early socialists try to live? how did they see and relate to one another? what did they think and feel about love, about their bodies and their sexuality? To demand so impertinently of the past is a political choice based on a redefinition of the relationship between what is political and what is personal and would require a reworking of the socialist past. It is more common in labour history to ask either how the working class has sought to take power or tried to improve their position within the framework of capitalism. The focus has been accordingly on moments of militancy, on the building of revolutionary organisations or on the defensive structure of the union and the growth of parliamentarianism. This has obscured the interior life of political movements of the working class and glanced over important aspects of the socialist tradition in which the transfer of state power and workers control of industry were not the aim but the means. The aim was the realisation of a society in which men and women could associate and create in love, beauty and freedom. For this the years of propagandising, the scraping up of money for the new club rooms, the pain of factional disputes could be borne. It is not to deny the importance of class power to say that this was not what moved many people to become socialists. The making of an alternative consciousness is a complex process touching strange places. When we look for a concern to transform all forms of social relationship in the past Edward Carpenter and his friends, shunted into the sidings as eccentric oddities, finally come out dusting down their utopian dreams.

Perhaps on close questioning some of these 'eccentrics' would have explained that they saw the means and the aim of socialism as inseparable. For Carpenter and for many socialists of his day the personal moral vision had a most significant reality and required immediate action. He became convinced that it was morally wrong for the privileged to live off the labour of the poor and was aesthetically repulsed by the ugliness and waste of capitalism. His socialism in the 1880s developed out of this sense of ethical wrong and romantic loss. It was a socialism inseparable from a vision of new life, of new growth finding roots, sharing with the romantics earlier in the century a conception of a natural humanity made monstrous by civilisation and a yearning for community which many nineteenth-century critics of capitalism from the utopian socialists to Ruskin had expressed. The dreams did not die even when the hope of revolution became dim. Carpenter's life and writing were connecting inspirations.

There was implicit in this socialism a feeling for spiritual and mystical insight. The work of changing the fabric of capitalist society was only one aspect of their struggle. The end was the new life and they carried its potential within them. A.R.Orage wrote to Carpenter in February 1896 of his and Whitman's influence. He told Carpenter of the popularity of *Towards Democracy* among readers of the ILP paper *The Labour Leader*.[255] It was still being read by a later generation. Fenner Brockway said *Towards Democracy* was read after propaganda outings and rambles and was regarded as a 'bible', the spiritual food of socialists.[256] *Love's Coming of Age* was also popular. It went through eleven editions between 1896 and 1919.

Of course spiritual food is one thing and sexual liberation quite another. It is difficult to know whether his audiences accepted all his ideas or whether they saw him as a vaguely poetic figure. But it is evident that many of his concerns were still part of the current socialist discussions even if the actual impact of these talks and of his writings on the radical movements of the 1890s and 1900s, the socialism of the Independent Labour Party and Clarion and the suffragettes is unclear. The attempt to follow his influence through systematically would undoubtedly provide interesting insights about the relationship of these movements to one another and the approach to sexual politics.

Certainly there were men and women within the socialist groups who identified closely with his ideas about the liberation of women. This was probably most true of the ILP. Lily Bell, for instance, writing in the Independent Labour Party paper *The Labour Leader* reviewed his work favourably in 1896. She said she felt that he was one of the few men who could write about sex and women without patronage:

Most men write with such an air of superiority, such an assumption of masculine authority and right to lay down the law as to what women may or may not do, what may or may not be her proper 'sphere', in life, that I usually take up their articles merely to lay them down with a feeling of impatience and irritation.[257]

There was certainly a current within the socialism of the 1880s and '90s prepared to discuss a changing relationship to the body as well as changed relations between men and women. Very little is known about this in Britain though and it appears to have been stronger within American radicalism. Besides Helena Born and Miriam

Daniell there was at least one other merging of the two traditions. An ex-Bristol socialist, Robert Allen Nicoll, who had emigrated to the West Coast of America and was a friend of Weare, Unwin, the Sharland brothers, Born and Daniell, wrote to Carpenter in 1894 remembering the house and the road to Chesterfield. He enthused in his letter about the liberatory effect of emancipating feet from shoes and asked Carpenter for sandals. 'One begins to own one's body at last.'[258] Two years later he wrote to tell Carpenter of a 'clear feeling . . . I could distinguish myself as something apart from and superior to my brain and intellect. There swept thro' [sic] me a power of mastery over my body – not an attitude of rejection, but self-realisation – something I have long known and believed but never up till now realised.' He added 'I want to realise my body and all its faculties.' Nicoll longed for a 'glorious comradeship, a band of brothers, men and women each with their art, who could co-operate'. He believed 'No longer can priest or anyone cast obloquy on the sexual act or on women, on the testes or vagina or womb, or the sweetness of coition.'[259]

There were also socialists hostile to any connection of socialism with sexual radicalism. Robert Blatchford, the editor of the popular paper *The Clarion*, expressed his disagreements with Carpenter in letters in December 1893 and January 1894. He was enthusiastic about *Civilisation. Its Cause and Cure* and the book about India *From Adam's Peak to Elephanta* but not about Carpenter's idea of writing about sexuality. Blatchford said he did not think our 'parts' should be displayed 'as sexual graces'. He did not find them beautiful. 'Perhaps I'm a predjudiced old Tory; but the whole subject is "nasty" to me.' He admitted that sexual relations must be altered but believed this must come after economic and industrial change. Feeling and prejudice were so strong about sexuality that 'if Socialists identify themselves with any sweeping changes in those relations the Industrial Change will be seriously retarded.' Blatchford believed 'the time is not ripe for Socialists, as Socialists, to meddle with the sexual question.'[260]

Carpenter's writing on homosexuality must have been the most difficult to accept for socialists like Blatchford who felt that socialism could be made by isolating the economic from personal and sexual relationships.

How far his opinions can be taken as shared by other leaders of the labour movement is uncertain. But the effort to become respectable as a parliamentary party must have created pressure to disassociate socialism from sexual questions. It was left to a later generation of sex reformers to take up these issues within the Labour Party. Equally the marxists at the centre of the SDF led by Hyndman were not likely to support even heterosexual love 'coming of age' in the immediate future.

Even the anarchists who were theoretically more disposed to discard political respectability and were sympathetic to free unions, sexual liberation and co-operative housework seem to have baulked at his ideas on homosexual love. Peter Kropotkin, who spoke at the Sheffield Socialist Club and belonged to the 'Freedom' group, was said to have 'rather turned up his nose' on hearing that Carpenter was working on a book 'dealing with friendship between two people of the same sex'.[261] David Nicoll, who conflicted with Carpenter over the defence of Fred Charles and the other Walsall anarchists, had by the 1900s become consumed with suspicion and convoluted fears of plots and spies. He continued to issue *Commonweal* on a sheet in which he expressed his terrors of Jesuit homosexual intrigues within the Independent Labour Party in which Carpenter was one of the most suspicious characters, responsible for the defeat of revolution, for the Jameson raid and for Morris' death. He saw homosexuality as an upper-class, clerical abnormality which led to 'nerve disease and ultimately insanity'. It should be treated by 'kindly restraint'.[262]

There was certainly also an extreme reluctance among the leaders of the women's suffrage movement to be associated with demands for sexual liberation.[263] It was therefore particularly embarrassing when O'Brien interrupted Carpenter at a suffrage meeting. Bertrand Russell described staying with Carpenter and Millicent Fawcett, the leader of the constitutional suffragists, in a house in Edinburgh during a suffrage conference. Fawcett refused to talk to Carpenter because of his writings on homosexuality which caused some embarrassment to the other guests.[264] Emmeline and Christabel Pankhurst, in the Women's Social and Political Union, were similarly concerned to concentrate on the vote and not to explore the sexual implications of feminism.[265] Carpenter was closest to Charlotte Despard, a socialist feminist. She had been a member of the SDF and ILP and the Pankhursts' WSPU until she became critical of the lack of internal democracy in the WSPU and broke away with other women to form the Women's Freedom League. They spoke together at a Trafalgar Square meeting and he took the chair for her in 1912 at a meeting of the Sheffield Women's Freedom League. Mrs Despard persuaded him to write for the League's paper *The Vote* in 1910.[266]

But his connecting inspiration was not so much at the centres of either socialism or feminism but in small local groupings. To follow Carpenter's effect through would thus also be one way of seeing an alternative reality to the picture presented by the national leaders. For instance the histories of socialism and feminism are usually presented as quite distinct. Historians follow the records of particular organisations. More popularly Sylvia Pankhurst's break with her mother and sister appears to confirm such a separation. Viewed from on top and through the journals this is probably accurate but the official version is not always what actually happened at a local level where theoretical, political, organisational and personal preoccupations jostle against one another.

There was undoubtedly considerable suspicion among the leaders of both the SDF and the ILP of the militant suffrage movement which emerged after Mrs Pankhurst broke from the ILP and formed the WSPU. This was partly a theoretical conflict: there was no basis in current socialist theory for an autonomous movement of women. Nor was there any understanding of the significance of the control of reproduction. The sexual division of labour was regarded as natural and conflict between the sexes tended to be subordinated to class conflict. The issue was confused politically by many of the suffragettes' insistence on the vote as an isolated reform and by Emmeline and Christabel's subsequent move to the right. A less official cause of rancour was understandably organisational and must have affected the branches more nearly. There was no doubt local competition for membership and fear among men in local socialist groups, whether SDF, Clarion, ILP or Fabians, that they would have to make concessions in order to retain their women members. The impact of the feminist movement on local socialist organisation remains relatively unexplored.[267] It would be surprising if it did not raise awkward questions of inequality within the movement. It was one thing to pronounce on the woman question and quite another to stay in while women went to meetings or for the men to do the domestic work for a social gathering.

Carpenter as an homosexual man was amused at male uneasiness about the women's assertiveness. In his notes on women's suffrage in 1908 he commented: 'Males [are] getting alarmed for their supremacy. And I sometimes think a good thing. They should be alarmed – stir them up a bit.' He was interested in the effect of the agitation on the women's consciousness. He said they were 'full of go and originality'.[268]

The implications of the suffrage movement on personal relations between the sexes must also have been considerable. Carpenter may have been distrusted by Mrs Fawcett and by Emmeline and Christabel Pankhurst as a dangerous connection, but he was still very important to women who were involved in the feminist movement. There were for example old friends like Isabella Ford in Leeds who worked both with the ILP and the suffrage movement.[269] There was still his popularity in the socialist movement around Sheffield. Jessie Stephen, a socialist feminist from Glasgow, describes discussions in her local WSPU of a wide range of questions which affected women, including divorce. She went to work for Sylvia Pankhurst's Workers' Suffrage Federation in the First World War. On her first tour for the Federation, which had groups in several towns besides the East End of London, she stayed with Mrs Marion in Sheffield and indicates how Carpenter's views were communicated:

The author, Edward Carpenter lived just outside Sheffield and Mrs Marion told me of her interest in his books. Her favourite was . . . 'The Coming of Love' [*Love's Coming of Age*]. Over this she would enthuse and recite passages from memory. In the socialist movement it was very widely read.[270]

The belief in women's personal freedom was certainly not confined to advanced young women in London. Florence Exten was a member of the WSPU in Southampton and the ILP later in Bristol. As a young girl she had been on Clarion cycle rides with her mother in bloomers, though they had to carry skirts to put over them when they went through towns. She was a clerical worker active in her union where she met Maurice Hann, a grocery assistant. Katherine Glasier, then a member of the Bristol ILP, used to call them 'the doves'. They considered a free union but decided to marry in the end.[271] Socialism meant questioning the whole range of social relationships.

In Eastwood, near Nottingham, there was a group of advanced men and women, socialists and feminists interested in sexual liberation, and new theories of art. Carpenter came to visit them among other socialist and feminist speakers. They read and discussed A.R.Orage's journal *The New Age*. There was a personal link between Carpenter and this group. Sallie Potter, sister of Joe Potter, the young man Carpenter used to watch run races in Sheffield, married William Hopkin, a cobbler. Sallie Hopkin and her friend Alice Dax supported the suffrage movement. They were also affected by the cultural aspects of feminism. Alice Dax had advanced views on dress, house decoration and tried to live Carpenter's 'simplification of life' as a rebellion against Victorian formality and hypocrisy. She was unhappy in her marriage and resentful towards men. She became involved in a love affair with the young D.H.Lawrence who was a member of this circle. She is portrayed in his character Clara in *Sons and Lovers*. She was friendly with Jessie Chambers and gave her *Love's Coming of Age* to read around 1909–10.[272] Jessie Chambers was presented by

Lawrence as Miriam in *Sons and Lovers*, a characterisation which hurt her and which she rejected as 'a fearful treachery'.[273] The existence of this Eastwood group has become known because of Lawrence's subsequent fame. But it would be surprising if it were completely unique.

Carpenter's impact must have been most felt among those socialists and feminists who were seeking some understanding of sexual relationships.[274] His writing was more accessible to them than Ellis's and important in connecting sexual liberation to their own politics. The existence of a feminist movement must have given his ideas on the position of women an immediate significance. Whatever effect he had it was largely despite the national leaders of both movements. But in small discussion groups like that in Eastwood men and women talked earnestly about socialism, about new theories of aesthetics, about feminism. Carpenter was part of this advanced thinking and his example in trying to live class and sex equality was noted and appreciated.

Carpenter's work was part too of a growing interest in sex psychology. In England the laborious studies of Ellis, the journal *The Adult* in the 1890s and a feminist journal *The Freewoman* in 1911 committed to creating a 'new morality' and including articles on subjects such as group living, homosexuality, as well as feminism, were signs of this interest. With his friend Laurence Housman, Carpenter founded the British Society for the Study of Sex Psychology in the First World War.[275] The intention was 'to question things that have not been questioned before'. The statement of aims announced firmly:

We mean to push our enquiry on the basis of men and women working fearlessly and frankly together over territory that is really common to both, but which, hitherto has been ridiculously cut up, separated and divided.

Members of the society believed: 'that nothing concerning sex can be rightly dealt with by one sex deciding and acting alone, and that in consequence of decisions so formed and so acted on society is suffering today'.[276]

They found signs of sexual confusion in the state of marriage and divorce, the spread of VD and the lack of sex education. They believed in the economic right of women to have children without being tied to a man. The subjects of the talks which followed included infantile sexuality, homosexuality, women's sexuality, and the play function of sex.

The influence of Carpenter's writing was at its height in the period before the First World War. It was international in scope. His books were translated into French, Dutch, Italian, Russian, Norwegian, Spanish, even Japanese. His ideas were influential in radical circles in Japan before the growth of marxism in the 1920s. His work was probably best known in Germany, where *Love's Coming of Age* sold around 40,000 copies after it was published in 1902, and in the United States.[277] In both countries there was a strong current seeking to connect sexual politics to socialism. In Germany, Magnus Hirschfeld founded the Scientific Humanitarian Committee in 1897, a pressure group for homosexual freedom. There was also discussion of questions of sexuality, birth control and abortion in the German left.[278]

In America, Greenwich Village became a centre for young intellectuals who sought to live in sexual equality. Carpenter and Ellis were read as exponents of the new morality. On the West Coast, where the influence of German marxism had never taken a hold, the old communitarian search for the new life persisted in new movements.[279] As late as 1932 T.H.Bell, an American anarchist friend, put out a pamphlet about Carpenter's ideas. It was published by the Los Angeles Libertarian Group.[280]

But really by this time Carpenter's reputation had waned, not only in America but elsewhere. His writing on sexuality appeared dated with the growth of psychoanalytic theory and greater sexual permissiveness. In the early 1930s Housman said his statements on homosexuality appeared to be too defensive.[281] Lowes Dickinson said of his writing 'To the young, who now discuss everything, these books may seem elementary.'[282] Carpenter died in 1929; his role as the prophet of ideal comradeship had become increasingly impossible in old age and he was too mischievous to accept the even more onerous role as a saint, being inclined to pinch the behinds of young adulatory visitors.[283]

It was not just that Carpenter grew older but that the world changed about him. Precisely why and how the preoccupation with various forms of personal transformation became increasingly severed from socialist politics requires massive historical investigation. It has been as ignored as the tradition in which they were regarded as inseparable. It needs to be pursued not only as a problem within the history of socialism but in relation to changes in capitalist society. It is more immediately possible to detect an aspect of this severing as an imaginative rent than as an historical process about which we as yet know very little. In microcosm the fiction of E.M.Forster and D.H.Lawrence carries uncanny echoes of Carpenter and his circle. Their sources were close to his two worlds, the liberal Cambridge intelligentsia with its Bloomsbury offshoots and the Midlands intelligentsia in Eastwood, socialists with advanced sexual and aesthetic views. The two writers' later work does not merely resemble Carpenter's ideas; it indicates the manner in which concern for personal relations changed by becoming detached from the active making of a socialist society. The two distinct responses of Forster and Lawrence to this separation mark boundaries of feeling which are often assumed to be fixed and inevitable, the inner and outer worlds are 'naturally' at variance. It is thus well to remember that they were not always thought to be so.

E.M.Forster knew Carpenter through their mutual friendship with G. Lowes Dickinson. Forster's novel *Maurice* was directly inspired by a visit to Millthorpe in 1913. It tells the story of feelings awakened in Maurice only to be betrayed by Clive who is accommodated into the respectable world and of the union between Maurice and Alec, a gamekeeper who is a Merrill type character in touch with his own desires.

E.M.Forster described how he came to write the book, which was not published until after his death, in a Terminal Note:

George Merrill . . . touched my backside – gently and just above the buttocks. I believe he touched most people's. The sensation was unusual and I still remember it, as I remember the position of a long vanished tooth. It was as much psychological as physical. It seemed to go straight through the small of my back into my ideas, without involving my thoughts. If it really did this, it would have acted in strict accordance with Carpenter's yogified mysticism, and would prove that at that precise moment I had conceived.[284]

Carpenter's attempt to express his homosexual feelings openly and freely was important to Forster. He too considered how love could be non-exclusive and uncorrupted by social restraint.[285] Forster was attracted also to other aspects of Carpenter's thought. They shared a fascination with India. Revulsion against the arrogance of English colonialism and the desire to learn from Indian culture are evident in Forster's *A Passage to India*. Forster understood Carpenter's mystical preoccupations. They both longed for the awakening of feeling. Forster said of Carpenter 'he touched everyone everywhere'.[286] In Forster's morality denial of such feeling, immersion in maintaining the world of external restraints, creates an emptiness, a vacancy filled by material concerns. Both were scrupulous in acknowledging the new aspirations of women but kept their real passion for new relations between men. Forster wanted men to be able to express love from the heart and he wanted this to transcend the race and class divide.

Forster's concealment of the physical aspect of male love gives a strangely hemmed-in intensity to his writing. Perhaps in the end it congeals his creativity. The strain of carrying physical passion within, revealing it only in a hint, a touch, a caress, a glance, a slight movement, is both considerable and debilitating.

This and the political changes which left Forster with a separation between personal relationships and external political action contribute towards a profound sense of helplessness about politics which is in marked contrast to Carpenter's passionate engagement and persistent efforts at connecting.

Forster noted sadly that Carpenter would be remembered by students of the late nineteenth century and early twentieth century:

for his courage and candour about sex, particularly about homosexuality, for his hatred of snobbery while snobbery was still fashionable; for his support of Labour before Labour wore dress-clothes; and for his cult of simplicity.[287]

Such connections seemed no longer possible. Not only were sexual and personal longings denied by labour leaders, the outer world seemed harder to change. Better to dwell calmly with the life within and trust only in the enlightened few. Leave the fabric of England with the man of the underdeveloped heart. But slowly this closed some of the openings Carpenter had revealed. Carpenter had grandly embarked on prophecy. Forster less grandly took cover in fantasy[288] and made a dignified retreat taking refuge in the orderly world of a Cambridge college where privilege and beauty have come to a long-standing arrangement. But the memory of Merrill's touch never quite went away.

D.H.Lawrence appears at first sight to be a very different aesthetic and political figure from Forster. So it seems curious to find echoes of Carpenter in both writers. Yet there are similarities in their insistence on an inner force shaping the outer forms of life, the interest in wordless communications, the rejection of machine civilisation, and loathing of what capitalism did to the countryside and its culture. Lawrence was also as preoccupied with personal relationships as Carpenter and Forster. His concern was part of his opposition to the numbing effect of industrialisation though he expressed it differently. He wanted people to be more in touch with one another, to be more alive.

Like Carpenter and Forster, he was extremely conscious of the personal implications of the feminism which was part of the radicalism he knew in Eastwood. Olive Schreiner's *Story of an African Farm*, for example, moved him greatly. Planning *The Rainbow* and *Women in Love* in 1912 he wrote to Carpenter's feminist friend Sallie Hopkin. 'I shall do a novel about Love Triumphant one day. I shall do my work for women better than the Suffrage.'[289] His assertion of the inner change in feeling over politics was characteristic. But it could still be contained within a radical context. Later he went further and further away from movements which sought to change the external forms at all until he came to see personal change as a substitute. He became hostile to all political movements, especially feminism, which he challenged explicitly in his portrayals of women.[290] But behind the myth of femaleness which he asserted in his books was the reaction to the tremendous personal and cultural impact of contemporary feminism. The women in his novels still have imaginative force while the historical movement they came out of has gone.

If he rejected feminism he was still not happy with relations between men. Gerald in *Women in Love* is Carpenter's ungrown man while Birkin is the seer, the Urning with both masculine and feminine characteristics.[291] Lawrence toys with the notion of physical love between men and draws back.[292] His 'soul trembles' at the merging and mingling.[293] Instead he explored the idea of a loving fellowship between men which recognised difference. Lawrence, like Carpenter and Forster, is happier with his men than his women. But unlike them he was concerned to assert the new relationship between men *against* the cultural changes of feminism. Carpenter saw changes within men as part of the liberation of women. For Lawrence they are inner bonds, the means of thwarting the new woman along with the machine world. These themes are clear in *Kangaroo* and *The Plumed Serpent* where a new religion of the old gods is created by an *elite* of enlightened men. The anti-democratic aspects of Carpenter's androgynous seer, latent in Forster, are more polarised and explicit in Lawrence.

Nonetheless Lawrence remains politically ambiguous. He understood Carpenter's pursuit of a new way of life, his desire to liberate human beings from external systems which confined them.[294] However estranged from twentieth-century socialism, the community building of the American utopians, the communitarians in the Sheffield area, Carpenter's schemes for simplification and the old dream of perfectibility still go with him. He wrote to William Hopkin in 1915, 'Get me a few people in Sheffield will you – people who care vitally about the freedom of the soul.'[295]

In his later wanderings in pursuit of an aristocracy of the soul he was perhaps still searching for his ideal colony. He continued to want a renewal of feeling and more open relationships between people of different classes and between men and women. Nor did he completely forget Sheffield; the first draft of *Lady Chatterley's Lover* was originally called *Tenderness*. The gamekeeper is called Parkin and he leaves the Chatterleys to become a factory worker and secretary of the Communist League in Sheffield.[296]

Forster and Lawrence's journeys away from the connecting circle of Millthorpe are not coincidental. Within their individual wanderings we can catch a glimpse of a wider social and political process. Carpenter's socialism had still contained an earlier utopian impulse. This kind of socialism died as capitalism developed. Ethical aspirations were assimilated by the Labour Party and became part of gradualist socialism. The impact of 1917 secured the hegemony of Leninism as a theory of revolution which was dismissive of the subjective personal quest and of the cultural creativeness of the earlier tradition. Edward Carpenter grew a little weary in old age waiting for England to arise and was inclined to grumble it was being a long time about it. For later generations the connection he assumed became harder and harder to imagine. E.M.Forster should have the last word for he observed Carpenter's disappointment with sympathy though he could not make the same political connections himself.

He said that Carpenter loved 'manual work' and 'fresh air' most of all and dreamed like Morris that their union would cure civilisation.

The labour movement took another course, and advanced by committee meetings and statistics towards state-owned factories attached to state-supervised recreation grounds. Edward's heart beat no warmer at such joys. He felt no enthusiasm over municipal baths and municipally provided bathing drawers. What he wanted was 'News from Nowhere' and the place that is still nowhere, wildness, the rapture of unpolluted streams, sunrise and sunset over the moon, and in the midst of these the working people whom he loved, passionately in touch with one another and with the natural glories around them. Perhaps labour will listen to him in the end. 'Who shall command the heart?' as he wrote himself.

It is well to remember that there are several potentialities in human nature, not one, and though it is possible to organise, organise, organise, which is all that political parties do at present, it is also possible to obey the heart's commands. If labour ever changes its course, he will come into his own, and if, as he maintained, his spirit continues to haunt the places and people he loved he will pass a happy little day in the midst of his immortal bliss.[297]

### References

1. Edward Carpenter, *My Days and Dreams*, 3rd ed London, Allen & Unwin 1918 p.321. (1st ed 1916.)

2. *ibid.*, p.15.

3. *ibid.*, p.14.

4. *ibid.*, p.42.

5. *ibid.*, pp.30–31.

6. *ibid.*, p.32.

7. *ibid.*, p.43.

8. *ibid.*, p.49.

9. *ibid.*, p.30.

10. *ibid.*, p.58.

11. Edward Carpenter, Sermon Notes, Mss *c.* 1870–71 (Carpenter Collection, Sheffield City Libraries).

12. *ibid.*

13. *ibid.*

14. Edward Carpenter, *Sketches from Life in Town and Country*, London 1908, pp.89–90.

15. Carpenter, *My Days and Dreams*, p.62.

16. *ibid.*, p.62.

17. Edward Anthony Beck to Edward Carpenter, quoted in Dilip Kumar Barua, 'The Life and Work of Edward Carpenter', Sheffield Ph.D thesis 1966. p.248.

18. Matthew Arnold to Arthur Hugh Clough, 12 February 1853, quoted in Wilfred Stone, *The Cave and the Mountain*, London, Oxford University Press 1966, p.9. See generally Walter E. Houghton, *The Victorian Frame of Mind* and Barua, 'The Life and Work of Edward Carpenter', pp.235–239.

19. Alfred Lord Tennyson, 'In Memoriam', in *The Poetical Works of Lord Tennyson*, London, Collins n.d. pp.370–371.

20. Walt Whitman, 'Calamus, In Paths Untrodden', in Walt Whitman, *Leaves of Grass*, London, Everyman 1957, p.97.

21. Walt Whitman, 'Children of Adam, I am he that aches with Love', *ibid.*, p.95.

22. Edward Carpenter to Walt Whitman, 12 July 1874 quoted in Barua, 'The Life and Work of Edward Carpenter', pp.66–69.

**23.** E.M.Forster, 'Book Talk: The Life and Works of Edward Carpenter' (broadcast talk, 25 September 1944).

**24.** Edward Carpenter to Charles Oates, 16 April 1877 (Carpenter Collection).

**25.** Edward Carpenter, Materialism, Mss notes of a lecture to Leeds Co-operative Society, 22 November 1874; Edward Carpenter, Pioneers of Science, Mss notes of 12 lectures 1879; Edward Carpenter, Science and History of Music, Mss notes of a lecture given to Nottingham Social Guild, 3 March 1880, and Sheffield Secularist Society, 17 February 1884 (Carpenter Collection).

**26.** Edward Carpenter, Autobiographical Notes, Mss (Carpenter Collection).

**27.** *The Sheffield Weekly Echo*, 31 November 1885.

**28.** Carpenter, *My Days and Dreams*, p.105.

**29.** *ibid.*, p.115.

**30.** Edward Carpenter, 'Co-operative Production with reference to the Experiment of Leclaire', a lecture given at the Hall of Science, Sheffield, Sunday 18 March 1883 (Alf Mattison Collection, Brotherton Library, Leeds University).

**31.** Olive Schreiner to Edward Carpenter, 5 September 1887 (Carpenter Collection). (I owe this reference to Ruth First.) For short accounts of Olive Schreiner's life and ideas see Ann Scott's interview with Ruth First, 'Olive Schreiner', *Spare Rib*, No. 29, and Sheila Rowbotham, *Women, Resistance and Revolution*, London, Allen Lane 1972, Pelican 1974, pp.92–96.

**32.** G. Lowes Dickinson to C.R.Ashbee, 2 May 1885 (Lowes Dickinson, *Letters*, King's College, Cambridge).

**33.** G. Lowes Dickinson to C.R.Ashbee, 23 January 1885, *ibid.*

**34.** G. Lowes Dickinson to C.R.Ashbee, quoted in C.R.Ashbee, *Memoirs*, vol. I, May 1885 (Mss Victoria and Albert Museum), p. 14.

**35.** C.R.Ashbee, *Memoirs*, *ibid.*, pp.5–7.

**36.** Stephen Winsten, *Salt and his Circle*, London, Hutchinson, 1951, p.64.

**37.** *Commonweal*, January 1886.

**38.** C.R.Ashbee, *Memoirs*, vol. I, pp.18–20.

**39.** G. Lowes Dickinson to Charles Ashbee, 11 February 1886 (Lowes Dickinson, *Letters*).

**40.** Gilbert Beith, *Edward Carpenter. In Appreciation*, London, G. Allen & Unwin 1931, p.36.

**41.** See Carpenter, *My Days and Dreams*, p.125; *Commonweal*, 1 May 1886; C.R.Ashbee, *Journal*, 30 March 1886.

**42.** *Sheffield Weekly Echo*, 14 August 1886; on Unwin, see Walter L. Creese, *The Legacy of Raymond Unwin, A Human Pattern for Planning*, Massachusetts, MIT 1967, p.1, pp.8–11.

**43.** *Sheffield Weekly Echo* (cutting in Carpenter Collection).

**44.** Sheffield Socialist Society 1886 (Mattison Collection).

**45.** D.Barua, 'Edward Carpenter and the Sheffield Socialists', *Transactions of the Hunter Archaeological Society*, No. 10, p.59.

**46.** Carpenter, *My Days and Dreams*, p.130.

**47.** *ibid.*, p.131.

**48.** *Sheffield Weekly Echo*, 14 November 1885, 12 December 1885, 21 August 1886.

**49.** *Commonweal*, 2 April 1887.

**50.** Carpenter, *My Days and Dreams*, p. 131.

**51.** Edward Carpenter to Charles Oates, undated letter, *c.* 1886–87.

**52.** Edward Carpenter, *Towards Democracy*, pp.394–395.

**53.** Carpenter, *My Days and Dreams*, p.131.

**54.** Edward Carpenter, Mss notes on George Merrill, 5 March 1913, p.28 (Carpenter Collection).

**55.** Carpenter, *My Days and Dreams*, p.131.

**56.** *Sheffield Independent*, 27 January 1932. On George Adams see Harold Armytage, 'George Adams, A Garden City Pioneer', *The Citizen*, Letchworth, 15 January 1932.

**57.** Carpenter, *My Days and Dreams*, p.131.

**58.** *Commonweal*, 28 August 1886.

**59.** *Commonweal*, 25 September 1886.

**60.** George Hukin to Edward Carpenter, January 1887 (Carpenter Collection).

**61.** *Sheffield Weekly Echo*, 26 February 1887.

**62.** *Sheffield and Rotherham Independent*, 23 February 1887 and *Sheffield Weekly Echo*, 26 February 1887.

**63.** E.P.Thompson, *William Morris, Romantic to Revolutionary*, London, Lawrence & Wishart 1955, p.568.

**64.** George Hukin to Edward Carpenter, 14 November and 21 November 1887 (Carpenter Collection).

**65.** George Adams to Edward Carpenter, 17 November 1887 (Carpenter Collection).

**66.** George Hukin to Edward Carpenter, 21 November 1887 (Carpenter Collection).

**67.** George Adams to Edward Carpenter, 24 November 1887 (Carpenter Collection).

**68.** Thompson, *William Morris*, pp.572–579 and pp.592–594.

**69.** George Hukin to Edward Carpenter, 14 November 1887 (Carpenter Collection).

**70.** George Adams to Edward Carpenter, 24 November 1887 (Carpenter Collection: catalogued wrongly as from George Merrill).

**71.** *Commonweal*, 10 December 1887.

**72.** George Hukin to Edward Carpenter, 11.30, Tuesday no date, *c.* December 1887 (Carpenter Collection: catalogued wrongly as from George Merrill).

**73.** *Commonweal*, 10 December 1887.

**74.** *ibid.*, 17 December 1887.

**75.** George Hukin to Edward Carpenter, 14 December 1887 (Carpenter Collection).

**76.** George Adams to Edward Carpenter, 11.30 Tuesday, no date, *c.* December 1887 (Carpenter Collection: catalogued wrongly as from George Merrill).

**77.** *Commonweal,* 10 December 1887.

**78.** *ibid.,* 17 December 1887.

**79.** George Hukin to Edward Carpenter, 15 March 1888 (Carpenter Collection).

**80.** Carpenter, *My Days and Dreams,* pp.135–136.

**81.** *ibid.,* p.136.

**82.** *Sheffield Independent,* 27 January 1932.

**83.** Thompson, *William Morris,* p.479.

**84.** On new unionism see Hobsbawm, 'General Labour Unions in Britain 1889–1914', in E.J.Hobsbawm, *Labouring Men,* London, Weidenfeld and Nicolson 1964, pp.181–184. Also, H.J.Fryth and H.Collins, *The Foundry Workers, A Trade Union History,* Manchester, Amalgamated Union of Foundry Workers 1959, pp.89–98; and on the miners, J.E.Williams, *The Derbyshire Miners,* London, Allen & Unwin 1962, pp.298–306.

**85.** Williams, *The Derbyshire Miners,* pp.310–331.

**86.** George Hukin to Edward Carpenter, 16 January, 27 January 1889 (Carpenter Collection).

**87.** Edward Carpenter to James Brown, 23 April 1889 (Carpenter Collection); Edward Carpenter to Kate Salt, 9 April 1889 (Carpenter Collection).

**88.** George Hukin to Edward Carpenter, 7 July 1889 (Carpenter Collection).

**89.** For a longer account of the anarchists in Sheffield see Sheila Rowbotham 'Anarchism in Sheffield in the 1890s' in Colin Holmes and Sidney Pollard (eds) *Essays in the Economic and Social History of South Yorkshire.* Sheffield, South Yorkshire County Council 1977.

**90.** Carpenter, *My Days and Dreams,* p.135.

**91.** Edward Carpenter to James Brown, 3 June 1889 (Carpenter Collection).

**92.** Carpenter, *My Days and Dreams,* p.131.

**93.** *ibid.,* pp.134–135.

**94.** Henry Snell, *Men Movements and Myself,* quoted in Peter Wyncoll, 'The Early Socialists in Nottingham', *Marxism Today,* August 1973, p.242.

**95.** Samson Bryher, *An Account of the Labour and Socialist Movement in Bristol,* Bristol 1929, p.24.

**96.** *ibid.,* p.25.

**97.** *ibid.,* p.5.

**98.** *ibid.,* p.100.

**99.** Helena Born 'The Last Stand against Democracy', in Helen Tufts, *Whitman's Ideal Democracy,* Boston, Mass., Everitt Press 1902, p.74.

**100.** Tufts, *Whitman's Ideal Democracy,* p.44.

**101.** *ibid.,* p.xvi.

**102.** Alf Mattison's Letter book (E.P.Thompson).

**103.** Tufts, *Whitman's Ideal Democracy*, p.xvi.

**104.** *ibid.*, p.xvii.

**105.** *ibid.*, p.xx.

**106.** *ibid.*, p.xx.

**107.** Wilfred Whitley, *J. Bruce Glasier, A Memorial*, London 1920, p.9, quoted in Stanley Pierson, *Marxism and the Origins of British Socialism*, Ithaca N.Y., Cornell University Press 1973, p.146.

**108.** Laurence Thompson, *The Enthusiasts. A Biography of John and Katharine Bruce Glasier*, London, Gollancz 1971, p.81.

**109.** *ibid.*, p.82.

**110.** *ibid.*, p.65.

**111.** Beith, *Edward Carpenter. In Appreciation*, p.83.

**112.** *ibid.*, p.86.

**113.** *ibid.*, pp.84–85.

**114.** Tufts, *Whitman's Ideal Democracy*, p.xvi.

**115.** *ibid.*, p.xviii.

**116.** *ibid.*, p.xviii.

**117.** *ibid.*, p.xix.

**118.** E.P.Thompson, 'Homage to Tom Maguire' in Asa Briggs and John Saville (eds), *Essays in Labour History*, London, Macmillan 1960, p.298.

**119.** *ibid.*, p.313.

**120.** Alf Mattison, Notebook I, pp.25–26 (Mattison Collection). I owe this reference to Gloden Dallas. For a description of socialist culture in the Clarion movement see Logie Barrow, 'The socialism of Robert Blatchford and the Clarion newspaper, 1889–1914', University of London, Ph.D. thesis 1975.

**121.** Charles F. Sixsmith, Memories of Edward Carpenter (Sixsmith Collection, John Rylands University Library of Manchester).

**122.** George Hukin to Edward Carpenter, 8 July 1886 (Carpenter Collection).

**123.** Winsten, *Salt and His Circle*, p.76.

**124.** Alf Mattison, Mss notes on Edward Carpenter (Carpenter Collection).

**125.** Beith, *Edward Carpenter. In Appreciation*, p.216.

**126.** *ibid.*, pp.180–187.

**127.** George Hukin to Edward Carpenter, 21 May 1887 (Carpenter Collection).

**128.** *ibid.*, 15 May 1887.

**129.** *ibid.*, 21 May 1887.

**130.** *ibid.*, 24 May 1887.

**131.** George Hukin to Edward Carpenter, Whit Sunday 1887; Edward Carpenter to George Hukin, Whit Monday 1887; George Hukin to Edward Carpenter, 1 June 1887 (Carpenter Collection).

**132.** *ibid.*, 21 November 1887 (Carpenter Collection).

**133.** *ibid.*

134. *ibid.*

135. Carpenter, 'Philolaus to Diocles', *Towards Democracy*, p.394.

136. Carpenter, 'In the Stone Floored Workshop', *Towards Democracy*, p.394.

137. Edward Carpenter to Charles Oates, 19 December 1887, quoted in D.K.Barua, 'The Life and Work of Edward Carpenter', p.254.

138. Beith, *Edward Carpenter. In Appreciation*, p.155.

139. Edward Carpenter to James Brown, 23 April 1889 (Carpenter Collection).

140. *ibid.*, 3 June 1889.

141. *ibid.*, 16 January 1890.

142. *ibid.*, 2 March 1890.

143. Carpenter, *My Days and Dreams*, p.159.

144. Edward Carpenter, Mss, Notes on George Merrill, 5 March 1913 (Carpenter Collection), p.2.

145. *ibid.*, p.5.

146. *ibid.*, p.12.

147. *ibid.*, p.14.

148. *ibid.*, pp.16–18.

149. *ibid.*, p.20.

150. Carpenter, *My Days and Dreams*, p.160.

151. Carpenter, Mss, Notes on George Merrill, p.22.

152. *ibid.*, pp.29–31.

153. Edward Carpenter, 'Haziz to the Cupbearer' in *Towards Democracy*, p.393.

154. Carpenter, *My Days and Dreams*, p.160.

155. *ibid.*, p.161.

156. *ibid.*, pp.162–163.

157. Tom Barcley, *Memoirs and Medleys. The Autobiography of a Bottle Washer 1852–1933*, Leicester, Edgar Backus 1934, p.85.

158. Charles Sixsmith, Mss, Memories of Edward Carpenter (John Rylands University Library of Manchester), p.9.

159. Carpenter, *My Days and Dreams*, p.163.

160. *ibid.*, p.162.

161. Mrs Havelock Ellis, *Personal Impressions of Edward Carpenter*, Berkeley, The Free Spirit Press 1922, pp.11–12.

162. Beith, *Edward Carpenter. In Appreciation*, p.168.

163. Carpenter, *My Days and Dreams*, p.163.

164. *ibid.*, p.160.

165. *ibid.*, pp.161–162.

166. *ibid.*, p.250.

167. Beith, *Edward Carpenter. In Appreciation*, pp.217–218.

168. Mrs Havelock Ellis, *Personal Impressions of Edward Carpenter*, p.12.

169. Carpenter, *My Days and Dreams*, p.226.

**170.** Henry Salt to Alfred Mattison, 26 August 1929 in Alf Mattison's Letter book (E.P.Thompson).

**171.** Beith, *Edward Carpenter. In Appreciation*, p.218.

**172.** Carpenter, *My Days and Dreams*, p.164.

**173.** *ibid.*, p.197.

**174.** The Sheffield Fabians *Annual Report*, 1907–8, records the meeting. The incident is recorded in M.D.O'Brien, *Socialism and Infamy.The Homogenic or Comrade Love Exposed*, pp.18–19 (Carpenter Collection).

**175.** O'Brien, *Socialism and Infamy*, pp.18–19.

**176.** Beith, *Edward Carpenter. In Appreciation*, p.109.

**177.** *ibid.*, p.143.

**178.** O'Brien, *Socialism and Infamy*, p.1.

**179.** *ibid.*, p.14.

**180.** *ibid.*, p.3.

**181.** *ibid.*, p.2.

**182.** *ibid.*, p.4.

**183.** *ibid.*, p.9.

**184.** *ibid.*, p.9.

**185.** *ibid.*, p.5.

**186.** *ibid.*, p.3.

**187.** *ibid.*, p.15.

**188.** *ibid.*, p.7.

**189.** George Hukin to Edward Carpenter, 26 March 1909 (Carpenter Collection).

**190.** *ibid.*, 12 March 1909.

**191.** *ibid.*, 26 March 1909.

**192.** *ibid.*, 11 April 1909.

**193.** *ibid.*

**194.** George Hukin to Edward Carpenter, 10 September 1909 and 18 March 1910 (Carpenter Collection).

**195.** George Hukin to Edward Carpenter, 8 February 1890 (Carpenter Collection).

**196.** *ibid.*, 26 February 1891.

**197.** *ibid.*, 11 November 1891.

**198.** George Adams to Edward Carpenter, 17 August 1887 (Carpenter Collection).

**199.** George Hukin to Edward Carpenter, 9 January 1893 (Carpenter Collection).

**200.** Edward Carpenter to Kate Salt, 7 March 1895 (Carpenter Collection).

**201.** *ibid.*, 16 April 1890.

**202.** *ibid.*, 6 May 1892.

**203.** George Hukin to Edward Carpenter, 14 July 1891 (Carpenter Collection).

**204.** *ibid.*, 11 November 1891.

**205.** *ibid.*, 25 July 1893.

**206.** Edward Carpenter to Kate Salt, 12 June 1894 (Carpenter Collection).

**207.** *ibid.*, 7 March 1895.

**208.** Carpenter, *My Days and Dreams*, p.151.

**209.** Edward Carpenter to Kate Salt, 12 June 1894 (Carpenter Collection).

**210.** Carpenter, *My Days and Dreams*, p.131.

**211.** Alf Mattison, Notes on Edward Carpenter (Carpenter Collection).

**212.** Alf Mattison Notebook I, p.44 (Mattison Collection).

**213.** Edward Carpenter, Mss, Notes on George Merrill, p.5 (Carpenter Collection).

**214.** Edward Carpenter to George Hukin, 29 June 1901 (Carpenter Collection).

**215.** Edward Carpenter, Mss, Notes on George Merrill, p.13 (Carpenter Collection).

**216.** Alf Mattison, Notes on Edward Carpenter (Carpenter Collection).

**217.** 'Our Local Pioneers', Florence Mattison, 30 May 1947, newspaper cutting in Alf Mattison's Letter book (E.P.Thompson).

**218.** Beith, *Edward Carpenter. In Appreciation*, p.187.

**219.** *ibid.*, p.211.

**220.** Edward Carpenter to Alf Mattison, 1911. Alfred Mattison, Notebook II, p.5. (Mattison Collection). I owe this reference to Gloden Dallas.

**221.** Kate Salt to Edward Carpenter, 5 February 1889 (Carpenter Collection).

**222.** *ibid.*, 4 June 1892.

**223.** *ibid.*, 17 February 1897.

**224.** Winsten, *Salt and His Circle*, p.9.

**225.** Carpenter, *My Days and Dreams,* pp.321–322.

**226.** Carpenter, *Towards Democracy*, p.37.

**227.** *ibid.*, p.18.

**228.** *ibid.*, p.46.

**229.** *ibid.*, p.31.

**230.** *ibid.*, p.50.

**231.** *ibid.*, p.48.

**232.** Edward Carpenter, *Civilisation. Its Cause and Cure*, 3rd ed London 1893, p.11. (1st ed 1889.)

**233.** Carpenter, *My Days and Dreams*, p.248.

**234.** See Keith Neild, 'Edward Carpenter, Socialist and Author' in *Dictionary of Labour Biography*, vol. II, London, Macmillan 1974, p.89, and Carpenter, *My Days and Dreams*, pp.261–263.

**235.** Edward Carpenter, 'The Larger Socialism', Lecture notes 1909–10 (Carpenter Collection).

**236.** Barua, 'The Life and Work of Edward Carpenter', p.209.

**237.** See Richard Maurice Bucke, *Cosmic Consciousness*, London, Olympia Press 1972, pp. 188–206.

**238.** Barua, 'The Life and Work of Edward Carpenter', p.192.

**239.** Edward Carpenter, 'Empire' in Bruce Glasier (ed), *The Minstrelsy of Peace*, London, National Labour Press *c.* 1918.

**240.** Barua, 'The Life and Work of Edward Carpenter', p.195.

**241.** See Edward Carpenter, *Visit to a Gnani*, 2nd ed London 1920, pp.17–28.

**242.** Barua, 'The Life and Work of Edward Carpenter', pp.183–187.

**243.** *ibid.*, pp.202–207.

**244.** Edward Carpenter, *Love's Coming of Age*, 10th ed London 1918, pp.34–55.

**245.** *ibid.*, p.52.

**246.** *ibid.*, p.56.

**247.** *ibid.*, p.83.

**248.** *ibid.*, pp.196–197.

**249.** See Raymond Lee Muncy, *Sex and Marriage in Utopian Communities, Nineteenth Century America*, Baltimore, Penguin, pp.160–170.

**250.** Carpenter, *Love's Coming of Age*, p.172.

**251.** See Graeme Woolaston, *Edward Carpenter* (LSE Gay Culture Society pamphlet), and Jeffrey Weeks's chapter on 'Edward Carpenter and friends', in his forthcoming book on homosexuality.

**252.** Edward Carpenter, *Some Friends of Walt Whitman. A Study in Sex Psychology*, London, British Society for the Study of Sex Psychology Papers 1924, p.14.

**253.** *ibid.*, p.14.

**254.** Carpenter, *Love's Coming of Age*, p.88.

**255.** A.R.Orage to Edward Carpenter, 3 February 1896 (Carpenter Collection).

**256.** Fenner Brockway, *New Leader*, 5 July 1929.

**257.** Lily Bell, 'Matrons and Maidens', *The Labour Leader*, 27 June 1896.

**258.** Robert Allen Nicoll to Edward Carpenter, 28 December 1894 (Carpenter Collection).

**259.** Robert Allen Nicoll to Edward Carpenter, March 1896 (Carpenter Collection).

**260.** Robert Blatchford to Edward Carpenter, 11 January 1894 (Carpenter Collection).

**261.** F.H.Bell, *Edward Carpenter, the English Tolstoy*, Los Angeles, The Libertarian Group 1932, p.15.

**262.** *Commonweal*, September 1902 and Good Friday 1909 (I owe this reference to John Quaill).

**263.** On the constitutionalists' attitude to sexual politics, see Leslie Garner's forthcoming London Ph.D. thesis, and Constance Rover, *Love, Morals and the Feminists*, London, Routledge and Kegan Paul 1970.

**264.** Lord Russell to Mr Barua, 29 October 1964, quoted in Barua, 'The Life and Work of Edward Carpenter', p.223.

**265.** Rover, *Love, Morals and the Feminists*, pp.140–152.

**266.** Carpenter, *My Days and Dreams*, p.263 and Neild, *Edward Carpenter*, p.10.

**267.** See Sheila Rowbotham, *Hidden from History*, London, Pluto Press 1974, 2nd ed, pp.90–108. Marion Ramelson, introduction to *The Petticoat Rebellion*, London, Lawrence and Wishart 1972, pp.11–13. R.S.Neale, 'Working Class Women and Women's Suffrage' in *Class and Ideology in the Nineteenth Century*, London, Routledge and Kegan Paul 1972, pp.143–169. More detailed studies of this problem will undoubtedly emerge from local work on the feminist movement.

**268.** Edward Carpenter, 'Notes on Women's Suffrage' (Carpenter Collection).

**269.** I owe this information about Isabella Ford to Gloden Dallas and to letters from Isabella Ford to Alf Mattison in Alf Mattison's Letter book (E.P.Thompson).

**270.** Suzie Fleming and Gloden Dallas, 'Jessie', *Spare Rib*, No. 32.

**271.** Sheila Rowbotham, 'Interview with Florence Exten-Hann, *Red Rag*, No.5, pp.19–21.

**272.** Emile Delaveney, *D. H. Lawrence and Edward Carpenter. A Study in Edwardian Transition*, London, Heinemann 1971, pp.21–25.

**273.** Helen Corke, *D. H. Lawrence's Princess. A Memory of Jessie Chambers*, Ditton Surrey, The Merle Press 1951, p.33.

**274.** See for example the comments of a young feminist, Evelyn Sharp, who met him in 1914, Beith, *Edward Carpenter. In Appreciation*, p.208.

**275.** The British Society for the Study of Sex Psychology, *Policy and Principles*, London, 1917, p.7.

**276.** *ibid.*, p.14.

**277.** Neild, 'Edward Carpenter', p.90. I owe the information about Carpenter in Japan to Yashiko Miyake.

**278.** See John Lauritsen and David Thorstad, *The Early Homosexual Rights Movement*, New York, Times Change Press 1974, pp.10–11.

**279.** See June Sochen, *The New Woman in Greenwich Village 1910–1920*, New York Quadrangle 1972, and *Movers and Shakers*, New York, Quadrangle 1973. See also Linda Gordon's forthcoming book on the history of birth control, and Mari Jo Buhle, 'Women and the Socialist Party 1901–1914' *Radical America*, vol. IV, No. 2, February 1970, pp.36–58.

**280.** Bell, *Edward Carpenter, the English Tolstoy*.

**281.** Beith, *Edward Carpenter. In Appreciation*, p.109.

**282.** *ibid.*, p.37.

**283.** Michael Davidson, *The World, the Flesh and Myself*, London, Mayflower-Dell 1966, p.120. I owe this reference to David Widgery.

**284.** E.M.Forster, *Maurice*, London, Penguin 1975, p.217.

**285.** Stone, *The Cave and the Mountain*, p.85.

**286.** Beith, *Edward Carpenter. In Appreciation*, p.75.

**287.** *ibid.*, p.80.

**288.** Stone, *The Cave and the Mountain*, p.123.

**289.** Delaveney, *D. H. Lawrence and Edward Carpenter*, p.26.

**290.** See Kate Millett, *Sexual Politics*, London, Rupert Hart-Davis 1971, pp.237–294.

**291.** Delaveney, *D. H. Lawrence and Edward Carpenter*, pp.100–102.

**292.** D.H.Lawrence, 'Walt Whitman' in Roy Harvey Pearce ed, *Whitman, A Collection of Critical Essays*, p.16–17.

**293.** D.H.Lawrence, *Kangaroo*, London, Penguin 1954, pp.119–120.

**294.** Delaveney, *D. H. Lawrence and Edward Carpenter*, p.231.

**295.** *ibid.*, p.26.

**296.** Paul O'Flinn, *Them and Us in Literature*, London, Pluto Press 1975, p.31.

**297.** Beith, *Edward Carpenter. In Appreciation*, pp.78–79.

Part 2
**Havelock Ellis and the Politics of Sex Reform**
by Jeffrey Weeks

*Havelock Ellis*, as a medical student

Part 2
**Havelock Ellis and the Politics of Sex Reform**
by Jeffrey Weeks

### Early Life and Outlook

Havelock Ellis was the most influential of the late Victorian
pioneers of sexual frankness. Like Edward Carpenter he sought to
undermine the rigid and restrictive morality of what he defined as
Victorianism, and to break through the taboos on free discussion.
But where Carpenter's influence was largely through his lifestyle
('propaganda by deed') and personal following, Ellis's influence
spread through the reception of his books. In his numerous
publications on sex-psychology and morality he attempted to
document the vast variety of sexual expression and re-assert the
importance of sex in the lives of individuals and in society. Today
his major work, the multi-volumed *Studies in the Psychology of
Sex* (largely completed by 1910, but still to this day not published
in its entirety in Britain) seems a trifle old fashioned, a diffidently
elegant monument to past prejudice and ignorance. But to his
contemporaries it often seemed daring, even outrageous. His close
friend and ally, the American birth control pioneer Margaret
Sanger, confessed to feeling 'psychic indigestion' for weeks after
struggling through its forest of detail on sexual variety. And to
recent generations of admirers he has been seen as a 'sage of sex', a
prophet of the Edwardian sexual revolution, the first of the 'yeah-
sayers'. A creator, in other words, of modern ways of looking at
sex.[1]

That the praises might seem a little extravagant when we look
closely at his work is a measure of how far we have come in

liberalising sexual attitudes. But an examination of his life and work can still be of more than antiquarian interest. For his method of approach is still common amongst advocates of sexual reform; and many of his more dubious conclusions are still frequently heard, even on the left. It is only now, under the impact of the sexual liberation movements, that we can properly begin to understand the strengths and weaknesses of his work. For above all, Ellis was a pioneer of those seemingly radical approaches to sex which were successfully integrated into the so-called 'permissive society' of the 1960s. His work is one of the springs from which the broad stream of sexual liberalism has flowed with apparent effortless ease. Today we can begin to see that the resulting approaches to sexual freedom are not enough: they have to be questioned and challenged before a truly radical perspective on sexual liberation can be realised.

Henry Havelock Ellis was born in 1859, the year of Charles Darwin's *Origin of Species*. He was born that is, of a generation which, as George Bernard Shaw put it, 'begun by hoping more from science than perhaps any generation ever hoped before.'[2] Ellis's outlook was moulded in this period of the triumph of Victorian science and the developing reaction against its implications.

He was the son of lower-middle-class parents living in the London suburb of Croydon. His father was a merchant sea captain, at home for only about three months a year, more a visitor than a constant presence. In his absence, Ellis's mother played the dominant role in the young boy's life. She was an ardent evangelical Christian, a convert at the age of seventeen, who vowed never to visit a theatre in her life, and kept to the promise. Despite this she seems to have been a humane influence and Ellis early sloughed off the more rigid aspects of her faith. He read avidly and in his adolescence his reading of Renan's *Life of Jesus*, of Swinburne, and of Shelley made him agnostic. But agnosticism was not an easy option then, and his emotional and intellectual development produced an inevitable personal crisis, one typical in the 1870s in his class and generation.

The crucial formative period for Ellis was his stay in Australia for several years from the age of sixteen. His father took him on what was intended as a voyage round the world, but he stopped off in Australia, where he became a teacher (and at the age of nineteen a headmaster) in the bush. Here, in almost total isolation, he began to experience conflicts in his awakening sexual life and simultaneously in his spiritual outlook. He experienced to the full the conflicts between his emotional longings, his guilt, his waning religion, and the dogmatic harshness of the Victorian ideologies of science, reduced to mechanical laws, outside human control. To the young Ellis the universe seemed a void, empty of all but money-making meaning.

This attitude, as he later wrote, was represented for him by David Friedrich Strauss's book *The Old Faith and the New*, a paean to Victorian science, published in 1872:

I had the feeling that the universe was represented as a sort of factory filled by an inextricable web of wheels and looms and flying shuttles, in a deafening din.[3]

Neither a religion that was dead, nor a science that had been completely absorbed into the capitalist-utilitarian denial of life, gave a purpose to the young man's life. It was at this point that Ellis read, for the second time, a book by James Hinton, a former doctor and ear specialist turned writer on political, social, religious and sexual matters, entitled *Life in Nature*. Hinton had developed a philosophy of life based on a pantheistic faith in the goodness of nature, in the unity of man with his surroundings. The book now produced in Ellis what he later called a 'revelation':

The clash in my inner life was due to what had come to seem to me the hopeless discrepancy of two different conceptions of the universe. On the one hand was the divine vision of life and beauty which for me had been associated with a religion I had lost. On the other was the scientific conception of an evolutionary world which might be marvellous in its mechanism but was completely alien to the individual soul, and quite inapt to attract love. The great revelation brought to me by Hinton ... was that these two conflicting attitudes are really but harmonious though different aspects of the same unity.[4]

The 'revelation' Ellis interpreted as a mystical experience. Though he henceforth rejected conventional religion, he was convinced that beyond the apparent gap between religion and science there was a basic unity and harmony to life. Although this now seems a typically Victorian semi-religious conversion, it provided Ellis with the inner strength with which he could confront the aridity of society, and offered a basis for his later philosophy. He became convinced that the meaning of life was a matter of individual perception; each person constructed for himself a pattern of meaning, in effect a myth. The construction of this interpretation was an art, and much of his later philosophical writing was to be concerned with the depiction of this 'Art of Life'. The dance most perfectly represented for Ellis the form of life: a unity of pattern, rhythm, feeling and intellect. And, as if to underline it, his first best-seller, published when he was already in his sixties, was called *The Dance of Life*. Such a view of life was the complete opposite of a materialistic analysis. but balancing this was his belief that science, directed by a humanist outlook, could lay bare the truth of human nature. In particular, for the young Ellis, Hinton's belief that sexual freedom would bring in a new age of happiness helped turn Ellis towards the study of sexual behaviour. A further reading of Hinton persuaded Ellis that the way to fulfilling his ambition to construct a new view of sex was to train as a doctor, to learn the established conventions of medicine before he began to challenge them. With this new faith and new ambition Ellis returned to Britain in the spring of 1880.

During the next decade he successfully trained as a doctor, finally qualifying in 1889, though he practised only sporadically thereafter. And he began to develop and express the wide range of his interests through writing: about literature (he edited a pioneering series of unexpurgated editions of English plays called 'The Mermaid' series), science (he began editing the influential 'Contemporary Science' series of books), religion, philosophy, travel, and politics. Above all, he entered in the early 1880s the heady world of radical political, moral and philosophical discussion that was emerging with the socialist revival. He met Hinton's family, who helped him through his medical training. Through his work on the radical journal *Today* he met H.M.Hyndman, the founder of the marxist Social Democratic Federation, and other early marxists. Through the Progressive Association of which he was secretary in the early 1880s, he became friendly with Eleanor Marx, and her lover Edward Aveling (translator of *Capital*). In the Fellowship of the New Life, of which he was a founder member, he established a close friendship with Edward Carpenter and other pioneering socialists. Above all, he began in the 1880s the two central emotional relationships of his early life, first with Olive Schreiner, and later with Edith Lees, who was secretary of the Fellowship's community house after Ellis had drifted away from the group, and whom he married. These contacts and personal relationships nourished his intellectual development and helped produce an outlook which could be defined in the fluid context of the 1880s as both socialist and feminist. In his first book *The New Spirit*, published in 1889, Ellis described what he saw as the 'spiritual awakening' of the age.[5] The chief elements of this were firstly, the growth of science; secondly, the rise of the women's movement; and thirdly, the march of democracy, demanding education and a 'reasonable organisation of life'. These elements became central parts of his outlook.

Nevertheless, in a conventional sense Ellis was never a political activist. In the early 1880s he acted as secretary to various discussion groups. Later, as a well-known writer, he worked with various organisations which aimed to promote more enlightened attitudes to sexual matters, such as the British Society for the Study of Sex Psychology, and he became in the 1920s a distinguished sponsor of the World Congress for Sex Reform. He gave his support to campaigns for birth control and abortion, and towards the end of his life, for voluntary euthanasia. But he was acutely shy, and never became deeply involved in public activity. His membership of an organisation or committee was always more nominal than real. His abiding interest was in exploring personal relationships and ethical concepts rather than in organising political campaigns.

This interest can be seen in the socialist organisations he was involved with in the early 1880s. The Progressive Association cultivated a tone of ethical uplift; for it Ellis edited a book of *Hymns to Progress* which had a distinctly inspirational quality. He wrote a hymn which sums up the spirit:

> Onward, brothers, march still onward,
> March still onward hand in hand;
> Till ye see at last Man's Kingdom
> Till ye reach the Promised Land.[6]

But it was the Fellowship of the New Life which most clearly represented Ellis's attitudes. He was one of its founders in the winter of 1883, and he helped draw up its constitution. According to this the Fellowship was to be based on the 'subordination of material things to spiritual', and aimed at 'the cultivation of a perfect character in each and all'. Through discussion, simple living, manual labour and religious communion, members hoped to lay the basis of a new life.[7] In early 1884, however, a split developed. Shaw, a leading protagonist, wrote later, 'Certain members of that circle . . . [felt] that the revolution would have to wait an unreasonably long time if postponed until they personally attained perfection.'[8] The dissidents split to form the Fabian Society, while the Fellowship followed its more individualistic path: 'one to sit among the dandelions, the other to organise the docks'.[9] Ellis stayed with the Fellowship (though with less and less involvement); its emphasis on the personal and spiritual suited his temperament better than the 'practical' and social engineering outlook of the Fabians. Nevertheless, in later years, his views can be loosely described as Fabian.

Ellis was familiar with many marxist ideas, but his socialism owed little to Marx and even less to the working class. In his book *The Task of Social Hygiene*, published in 1912, he rejected the revolutionary socialism of what he called the 'dogmatically systematic school of Karl Marx', and saw it, paradoxically on the eve of its greatest achievement, as a fading dream.[10] Given the organisation of English marxism under Hyndman, with its rigid determinism, so like the mechanical materialism that Ellis had early on rejected, and particularly its hostility to personal issues and feminism, this is not surprising. Instead he accepted the Fabian belief in the inevitable and gradual triumph of 'socialism' through the growth of large organisations and state control. However, this was for him but a means to an end. He advised the Fellowship in 1890 that we must 'socialise what we call our physical life in order that we may attain greater freedom for what we call our spiritual life'.[11] And as the utopian hopes for a rapid and total change nourished in socialist circles in the 1880s receded as the 1890s opened, Ellis like many others, adopted a more cautious tone and a political outlook which combined gradualism with individual self-cultivation. Like other late nineteenth-century radicals such as G.B.Shaw he found an inspiration in the work of the Norwegian playwright, Ibsen, whom he helped introduce to an English audience. In particular, he expressed his agreement with Ibsen's belief that the day of 'mere external revolutions' has passed, and that the only revolution now possible was the 'revolution of the human spirit'.[12]

Ellis was, with his brand of socialism, close to that 'humanist' ethical revolt against capitalism which has been a central strand in British radical thought in the absence of a developed historical materialism. Basic to it is the concept of a human essence, a true human nature, conceived of as basically good, whose full expression is thwarted and denied by 'civilisation' (as Carpenter called it), 'commercialism', or more straightforwardly, capitalism. In Ellis's view the 'essence' seems to have come close to being man's biological make-up, which had been distorted by capitalism and private property. Ellis's work here enters the whole debate about the nature of individuals, their relationship to society, and to the wider debate of 'nature' versus 'nurture'. Nowhere does Ellis more clearly reveal himself as a child of the age of Darwin. For an earlier age nature might seem vile and evil; but Ellis argued that, 'It must be among our chief ethical rules to see that we build the lofty structures of human society on the sure and simple foundations of man's organism.'[13]

Ellis shared with Carpenter and others a belief in the innate possibilities for good of man's biological nature: with him romanticism marries nineteenth-century scientific optimism in anticipation of a new enlightenment. But this is a central paradox of Ellis's work. The assumption that individual behaviour is an expression of inherent biological drives rather than of social processes tends today to be a hallmark of reactionary thought. For Ellis, however, it was the starting point of his radicalism. In this paradox lies the key to grasping Ellis's ambivalent position: he attempted to advance progressive arguments by methods which had an inbuilt limitation. For if social characteristics were given by nature there were limits beyond which social reform could not go. And it further suggested that change, to be successful, had to be gradual rather than radical, for it was constrained by inherent biological imperatives.

These biological assumptions come out very clearly in his study of *The Criminal* where, following Lombroso, he details the innate criminality of certain types of people; and in his work on *genius*, published in 1904, where he explores the inherent qualities in the limited number of people who reveal it. The implications of both these works are highly conservative, and have been largely discredited in the past half century, certainly among most liberals and radicals. But biological models of sexuality and sex roles have been much more persistent.

It was with relation to sexual affairs, Ellis believed, that 'man's organism' was most severely distorted by ancient prejudice and ignorance. With typical Fabian optimism he saw the traditional social problems — of religion and of 'labour' — as being on the road to solution. The sexual problem was for Ellis the outstanding remaining problem of the nineteenth century. After generations of war, revolution and counter-revolution in the present century, Ellis's optimism seems misplaced. It is, however, the crucial context for understanding his approach to sex reform. In the first revelation in the Australian bush he had envisaged himself as transforming attitudes to sexuality. By the 1890s he was more cautious; the work he now began to execute had a propagandist and educational tone, designed to produce long-term changes in attitudes. His most typical method was to assume an agreement in his audience and, as he admitted, be, 'quietly matter of fact in statements that at the time were outrageous'.[14] His aim was to begin to chip away the poison of the ages to allow men and women's real sexuality to emerge. It was with this approach that he began to produce his *Studies* and related works.

### Politics of Homosexuality

For Ellis, two areas of sex-psychology in particular needed exploration. The first was the question of sexual variations, what had, in western culture at least, traditionally been seen as 'sins' or 'perversions'. Homosexuality was the major example of these. The second area was the question of the relative social roles of men and women.

The first part of Ellis's *Studies* to appear was that dealing with homosexuality, *Sexual Inversion*, which was finally published in England in 1897. The troubles it immediately confronted clearly reveal the difficulties involved in discussing not only homosexuality but any sexual matter which did not conform to official stereotypes. It is therefore important to examine Ellis's treatment of homosexuality at some length.

It was Ellis's boast that he was one of the first to produce a major study of sex psychology which dealt with the 'normal' manifestations of sex as opposed, for example, to the work of the Austrian Richard Krafft-Ebing, whose massive *Psychopathia Sexualis* details sex in all its varieties, as a 'nauseous disease'.[15] On the surface therefore, it seems surprising that Ellis chose to open with a work on homosexuality. But the paradox is only a superficial one. He believed, indeed, that the so-called 'abnormal' manifestations of sex were often merely variations of the 'normal' mechanisms of sex, and that there was only a difference of degree between them. It is in this light, for instance, that Alfred Kinsey in his researches into sexual behaviour after the Second World War was able to recognise Ellis and Edward Carpenter as spiritual fore-bears, though he criticised them for lack of empirical accuracy. Equally important, Ellis recognised that of all the so-called 'devia-tions' homosexuality was closest in emotional terms to accepted heterosexuality, in that it provided the basis for close personal and sexual relations, just as heterosexuality did. Given this, the taboos against it seemed all the more dubious and Ellis recognised that an understanding of homosexuality was essential to the understanding of sexuality generally.

It was not until the last few decades of the nineteenth century that any attempt was made to conceptualise homosexuality as such. The pioneering work of homosexual rights campaigners, such as the German Karl Heinrich Ulrichs (1825–1895), found only a muted response in Britain. Traditionally, homosexuality had not been distinguished legally or morally from other forms of non-procreative sex. Legal prohibitions in Britain up to the mid-century had not identified a separate homosexual crime but had punished sodomy, the 'crime against nature', indifferently, regardless of whether between man and man, woman and man, or man and beast. Lesbianism as such was not recognised at all. Moreover, both in medical opinion and in the works of the social purity movement, homosexuality was little differentiated from masturba-tion, which, by inducing precocity of physical sensation, opened the gates to wickedness and 'lead inevitably to those terrors of unnatural vice which belong to disease not nature'.[16] It was the concept of homosexuality as a disease or mental illness which first grabbed the attention of 'medical authorities' who could then conceptualise homosexuality as a characteristic sign of individual mental derangement, derived from morbid ancestors or from corruption. Krafft-Ebing brought this trend to its peak by seeing homosexual behaviour as a fundamental sign of 'degeneration', and product of 'vice' working on 'tainted' individuals.[17] When Ellis first approached the subject there was no specific vocabulary in English for homosexuals separate from that of sin or disease – he was the first to use the word 'homosexuality', and to popularise the term 'sexual inversion', and 'invert'. And there was little empirical data of a neutral sort; not a single British case, unconnected with the asylum or the prison, had ever been recorded.[18]

But what made his work more than a theoretical effort but rather a political one was the new state of the law and public opinion. The death penalty for buggery – which had long fallen into disuse – had been abolished in 1861 but this was the prelude not to liberalisation but to a tightening of the laws against homosexuality. By a clause of the 1885 Criminal Law Amendment Act all sexual activities between men short of buggery were declared to be acts of 'gross indecency' punishable by up to two years' hard labour.

This Act, originally intended to raise the age of consent for girls to sixteen, and hence help control the 'white slave trade', was part of a series of measures passed in the late nineteenth century which had the effect of sharpening the division between 'legitimate' sex (sex between husband and wife within the family) and 'illegitimate' sex (sex which threatened the emotional stability of the family, and the socially sanctioned sexual roles of men and women). Homosexuality was seen as posing a threat to stable sexual relations within the bourgeois family, which was increasingly regarded as an essential buttress to social stability. Not surprisingly the late nineteenth century saw a distinct sharpening of social hostility towards homosexuality. The immediate result of the 1885 Act was a series of highly publicised court cases, which dramatised and accentuated the new mood. For homosexuals it meant an increased threat of social ostracism, a high incidence of blackmail, the threat of prison. In this furnace a modern homosexual identity was born.

Though not himself homosexual, Ellis had more than a theoretical interest in homosexuality from the start. He had, for instance, close friendships with homosexuals, such as Edward Carpenter; and above all his own wife, Edith, was lesbian. It has also been suggested that Ellis's own form of sexual variation, what he called 'urolognia' or 'undinism' – his sexual delight in seeing women urinate – made him more aware of the variety or 'naturalness' of sexual drives and the folly of trying to deny or obliterate them. But actually Ellis showed a relative indifference to the subject until the early 1890s. His book *The New Spirit* (1889) had contained a powerful essay on Walt Whitman, a strong influence on the ideas of personal liberation propagated by Carpenter and others, and had even compared him to Jesus Christ, which naturally shocked the bourgeois reviewers. But he passed over Whitman's theme of male comradeship, with its strong homosexual undertones, in relative silence.[19]

Nevertheless, the references had been enough to stir John Addington Symonds, a poet and critic, to write to Ellis, delicately broaching the subject of homosexuality; and by mid 1892, after a tentative correspondence they had agreed to collaborate on a study of 'sexual inversion'.[20]

Symonds himself was homosexual and had been exploring the new European theories concerning 'inversion' since the 1860s. He had already written for private circulation two pamphlets, *A Problem in Greek Ethics* and *A Problem in Modern Ethics*, concerning homosexuality in the ancient and modern world, and had conducted an extensive correspondence with Walt Whitman, culminating in a famous (and disingenuous) denial by the latter of his homosexuality. When he read Ellis's Whitman essay he had at first felt that here was a sympathetic soul (something that Symonds was always searching for); but their correspondence shows the development of a literary and intellectual rather than a personal relationship. The collaboration by letter – they never met – had a powerful impact on Ellis's views. He broadly agreed to work on the scientific aspects of the book, while Symonds contributed some case histories and historical notes. The aim was clearly propagandist as well as 'scientific'.

Ellis explained in a letter to Edward Carpenter the complex of aims behind the joint effort:

I have been independently attracted to it partly through realising how widespread it is, partly through realising also, how outrageously severe the law is in this country (compared with others) and how easily the law can touch a perfectly beautiful form of inversion. We want to obtain sympathetic recognition for sexual inversion . . . to clear away many vulgar errors – preparing the way if possible for a change in the law.

He concluded by stating that both he and Symonds were determined to put their own names to the book. Indeed, Symonds had insisted on this.[21]

But the political and social scene changed considerably between the conception of the book and its completion. The 1890s saw the evaporation of many of the millenarian hopes which had dominated the small socialist groups in the 1880s. The 1895 trial and downfall of Oscar Wilde, aesthete, utopian socialist and homosexual, symbolised for many the 'return of the philistines', the crushing of the more radical hopes of the 1880s for rapid and total change, and of the prospect of any swift changes in attitudes to sexuality. It particularly made the publication of a book on 'sexual inversion' a perilous matter.

Symonds died in 1893, but Ellis went ahead with the preparation of the book under joint authorship. A German edition appeared in 1896 and was favourably received in the medical press. Symonds had always spoken of the hazards of 'speaking out' on the 'great matter', and his *Memoirs*, written to reveal his attitudes and experience, and designed to educate the public opinion, had been suppressed after his death by his family; they remained under restriction in the London Library until 1976. Now, in the wake of the Wilde trial, the family panicked, and with the English edition already in print, Symonds's literary executor, Horatio Brown, bought up the whole issue of *Sexual Inversion*. Ellis was forced to agree to expunge all references to Symonds. But in attempting to bring out a new edition Ellis was faced with accumulating difficulties.

He had very cautiously attempted to have the book published as a medical treatise, preferring to work in accepted channels rather than risk confronting morality directly, but even this encountered strong opposition from the authorities. A friend of Ellis's, Dr Hack Tuke, whom Symonds had already judged 'unscientifically prejudiced to the last degree', had warned against publication, despite Ellis's protestations that it was for a specialist audience, by saying that there were 'always the compositors' who might be corrupted.[22] None of the orthodox medical publishers would take the book. As a result, more or less in desperation, Ellis accepted the offer of one Roland de Villiers, apparently a liberal-minded independent publisher to produce the English edition. Ellis seems to have naïvely been taken in by de Villiers, who was clearly less interested in the educational value of the work than in its commercial possibilities. Moreover, it later became apparent that he was a notorious confidence trickster, wanted by the police on the Continent and in Britain. With these inauspicious auguries, the second edition of the book, this time without Symonds's name on the title page, appeared in 1897. And almost immediately the book was drawn into an unexpected court case.

The book received a favourable response from the Legitimation League, a small society dedicated to sex reform, and in particular to advocating changes in the law relating to illegitimacy. Its magazine *The Adult* was published by de Villiers, and through him the Society came to display the book in its offices. Unfortunately for Ellis, Scotland Yard was keeping a close watch on the League, convinced it was the haunt of anarchists, then currently the terror of respectable London. The police obviously felt that a book on *Sexual Inversion* would provide a convenient hammer with which to crush the society.[23]

The secretary of the League, George Bedborough, was arrested, and eventually brought to trial in October 1898, for selling 'a certain lewd, wicked, bawdy, scandalous libel', namely Ellis's *Sexual Inversion*. Ellis himself was not charged nor indeed was the book itself on trial as such. A Free Press Defence Committee was established to defend free speech. Its membership reads like a roll-call of the political and literary left – Hyndman, Shaw, Carpenter, Belfort Bax, Grant Allen, George Moore; and the weather seemed set fair for a vigorous battle. But the case ended in anti-climax. Bedborough, under strong police pressure, was persuaded to plead guilty and was bound over. This had the effect of preventing anyone giving evidence on the book's merits. Ellis himself was never called to the stand, and the book, completely undefended, was labelled scandalous and obscene.

The case had important effects. In the first place Ellis

determined that future editions of his *Studies* would not be published in Britain. Thereafter they were printed in America, and to this day no full British edition of Ellis's most important work has appeared. In the second place, the police achieved a double victory: they crushed the Legitimation League as a supposed 'haunt of anarchists'; and they had effectively banned *Sexual Inversion* without even trying it on its merits (subsequently too they caught up with the publisher, de Villiers).

The case confirmed Ellis in his belief in the difficulties of changing attitudes. The 'crusade' he had vigorously advocated in his early work became more a subtle tilt at outrageous attitudes. He justified his caution in a famous pamphlet:

The pursuit of the martyr's crown is not favourable to the critical and dispassionate investigation of complicated problems. I must leave to others the task of obtaining the reasonable freedom that I am unable to obtain.[24]

Nevertheless, even this limited aim had its effect. The prosecution had in one major way been counter-productive: it publicised the book. As a result hundreds of homosexual men and women wrote to Ellis with their problems, their life histories, information and views. Many of these he was able to reassure; others he referred to Carpenter and other homosexual friends. Many of his correspondents found their way, as examples, into his books. Given the conspiracy of silence this was a major achievement. As Ellis said of the Wilde trial, publicity appeared 'to have generally contributed to give definiteness and selfconsciousness to the manifestations of homosexuality, and to have aroused inverts to take up a definite attitude.'[25]

Similarly, Ellis's work, like Carpenter's at the same time, greatly contributed to the sense of a homosexual selfconsciousness that becomes increasingly apparent from the 1890s. The contents of the book thus had a great impact on the ways in which homosexuals were labelled in the next generation or so; and is a crucial contribution to liberal views of homosexuality.

### 'Anomalies'

The aim of *Sexual Inversion* was to present a case for homosexuality, and its moral tone and method were the models for the later volumes of Ellis's *Studies* that dealt with sexual variations. The two principles he employed were a form of cultural relativism as applied to moral attitudes, and biological determinism as applied to essential sexual characteristics.

The first principle was useful in demonstrating the potentially transient nature of Victorian attitudes. By piecing together the anthropological, historical, religious and literary evidence that was available he attempted to demonstrate its common incidence: among animals (thus suggesting its 'natural' base to a generation gradually getting used to the idea that we were descended from the lower animals); amongst primitive peoples and in ancient civilisation; amongst famous literary and artistic figures; and in all social classes. His conclusion, written into his approach, was that homosexuality had always and everywhere existed; and in many cultures, indeed, it had been tolerated and even socially valued. Even in his own culture, he detected marked differences of attitudes between classes, with the working class relatively indifferent in attitude to the so-called 'perversions'.

Ellis's approach is still the most common amongst liberals in attempting to understand homosexuality: by collating all the available data, the aim is to show that it is not a product of particular national vices or periods of social decay, but a common and recurrent part of human sexuality. This is an important element in liberating our ideas of homosexuality. But in Ellis's case (and in that of most of his successors) it stopped there. No attempt was made to explore why forms of homosexuality were accepted in some cultures and abhorred in others, and the only hints he gave as to why homosexuals were oppressed in contemporary society were vague references to the survival of religious taboos. Ellis's approach is basically descriptive: the material roots are left unexplored.

Ellis was above all a naturalist, interested in recording 'facts' about human nature rather than judging them, or placing them into a coherent historical framework. It is said that his method was to collect information on a topic in an envelope until he had enough to write an article or piece on it. The result of this was to place a huge emphasis on what he regarded as the basic truth about homosexuality, its biological roots.

This was the second major element in Ellis's approach. The 'scientific' investigation of inversion was of recent date, and had developed in two distinct directions: one emphasising the acquired nature of homosexuality, the other its biological roots. The 'acquired' school had the disadvantage for reformers that it saw inversion as a vicious acquired *corruption*, evidence of national or personal decline. It pointed more to a moralistic clamp-down than to liberalisation. One of Ellis's case studies recounted that he first learnt of inversion in a class of 'medical jurisprudence' when it was classed with other non-normal acts as 'manifestations of the criminal depravity of ordinary or insane people'. The correspondent commented: 'To a student, beginning to be acutely conscious that his sexual nature differed from that of his fellows nothing could be more perplexing and disturbing.'[26] Biological arguments had the advantage of challenging this perplexity.

Ellis, like Krafft-Ebing, was prepared to accept that some homosexual predilections were acquired and in the final revised version of *Sexual Inversion* he made a distinction between 'homosexuality' which he defined as any sexual and physical relation between people of the same sex; and 'inversion' which was defined as a congenital condition. This implied that some people might indeed be 'corrupted' into homosexuality, and he was later to write in a typically liberal way, that it was the task of a sound social hygiene to make it difficult to acquire 'homosexual perversity'.[27] This opened up moral chasms and confusions that Ellis was never able to face. In the work of later would-be reformers in the 1950s and 1960s it led to some peculiar distinctions between 'inversion' which was regarded as 'natural', and therefore unavoidable and tolerable; and 'perversion' which was vice adopted by weak natures and therefore had to be condemned.[28]

Both 'inverts' and 'perverts' did the same things in bed, however, and the distinction relied on purely arbitrary judgements as to whether the homosexuality was inherent or acquired. And of course it implied that homosexual behaviour was only acceptable if it was involuntary and could not be suppressed. Havelock Ellis dodged this spongy ground by concentrating his arguments on congenital 'inversion'. This placed him in the main line of campaigners for homosexual rights, from Ulrichs through Edward Carpenter to the great German reformer, Magnus Hirschfeld (once fancifully called the 'Einstein of sex'); but distinctly apart from the work on sexuality that Freud was beginning at about the same time.

Havelock Ellis was deeply rooted in theories of the biological origins of human behaviour. His book, *The Criminal*, published in 1889, had been greatly influenced by notions of innate criminality derived from the Italian writer, Lombroso. The book, though dated, has an uncanny prevision of arguments current in the 1950s and 1960s, and still important today, that crime was essentially an abnormality, which could be treated like other illnesses. Several pieces of evidence convinced Ellis (he allowed himself to be easily convinced) that 'inversion' was similarly innate in homosexuals, and that most cases of acquired homosexuality on closer examination would reveal a retarded emergence of congenital tendencies. Firstly, he observed the 'strong impetus' in inverts which enabled them to defy conventional disapproval. This suggested to Ellis a drive which could only be examined as a fundamental element of the sexual instinct. Secondly, he noted the commonness of inversion in the same families, which again suggested to him its inherited nature. Finally, he observed its early appearance in most inverts. In his case histories, for instance, the average age of first same-sex attraction seems to be about nine. For Ellis this ruled out in most cases the possibility of environmental influences.

These are tenuous arguments which do not in the least rule out other explanations. But they had the propagandist advantage of allowing Ellis to reject current theories of 'degeneration', for a drive which was natural and spontaneous, he argued, could not simultaneously be a manifestation of a morbid disease.[29]

He took pains, therefore, to find a form of words describing homosexuality which did not suggest sickness, and the process can be traced in his correspondence with Symonds. Symonds originally felt that Ellis was too inclined to stick to 'neuropathical' explanations. Ellis countered this by suggesting that 'inversion' could best be seen as a technical 'abnormality', a congenital turning inwards of the sex drive, and away from the opposite sex. He rejected Carpenter's description of homosexuals as an 'intermediate sex', or 'third sex', feeling that it merely crystallised into a metaphor the superficial appearances. Struggling to escape the notion of sickness he suggested that perhaps 'inversion' could best be described as an 'anomaly', or a 'sport of nature'. Symonds was not so keen on 'sport' and suggested instead an analogy with colour blindness, which was a harmless variation. Ellis, in return, felt that even this might appear a deficiency, and suggested a comparison with colour-hearing, the ability to associate sounds with particular colours.[30] In this terminology inversion seemed less a disadvantage than a harmless quirk of nature.

He backed this up by carefully challenging certain stereotypes of homosexual behaviour, and even hinting at the moral excellence of 'inverts'. He particularly questioned the association of buggery with homosexuality, suggesting it was rare. The taboos against sodomy were still severe. Oscar Wilde had brought his disastrous court case against the Marquess of Queensbury after being accused of having 'posed as a sodomite' – 'posing' was enough! As Edward Carpenter put it, the law inhibited homosexual love by linking it with 'gross sensuality' and like Carpenter and Magnus Hirschfeld in Germany, Ellis deliberately played down this aspect for fear of jeopardising his reform aims.[31] This is a good example of the way in which Ellis was willing to temper his arguments (and tamper with the evidence) to get a foothold for reform. In the same way he attempted to challenge stereotypes of homosexual appearance. He denied, for instance, that most homosexual men were 'effeminate'; and he regarded transvestism as an essentially heterosexual phenomenon. Ellis was striving, in other words, to stress that 'inverts' were essentially 'ordinary' people in all but their sexual behaviour. This had the positive effect, on the one hand, of allowing him to challenge conventional misconceptions. For example, he denied that in homosexual relationships one person was always active, physically and emotionally, the other passive: 'Between men at all events, this is very frequently not the case, and the invert can not tell if he feels like a man or a woman.'[32]

This is an important point for it challenges the sexist assumption, still current, that homosexuals must pattern their relations on the stereotyped models of traditional male/female relations. But on the other hand, it had the danger, and one of which sexual liberals have rarely avoided, of imposing new standards of behaviour for the supposed 'deviant' which may be as restrictive, if more subtly so, as the old; it offers, for example, the possibility of being accepted as homosexual as long as you are suitably 'masculine' in appearance and manner. Such an approach does not, in the end, challenge sexist assumptions but helps to reinforce them.

Ellis was anxious, above all, to suggest the respectability of most homosexuals. He went to great lengths, for instance, to demonstrate that homosexuality was frequently associated with intellectual and artistic distinction. Some thirty pages of *Sexual Inversion* is devoted to homosexuals of note, including Erasmus, Michelangelo, Christopher Marlowe, Francis Bacon, Oscar Wilde, Walt Whitman, Sappho. Even here he showed a form of 'political tact': he carefully omitted names (like Shakespeare's) that might prove too controversial, and thus obscure his case. Again he established the pattern of later writers on the subject by bolstering up his case with long lists of distinguished names. The method unfortunately smacks strongly of tokenism, as if fame could give credence to behaviour, and leaves a slightly patronising air behind.

Of much more significance were the case-histories he gathered, some forty in all. They demonstrated much more effectively the moral, personal and intellectual quality of homosexual people, though he never went to the lengths of Carpenter, who tended to see the 'intermediate sex' as morally superior. The case-histories, often selected as he said from 'friends' (amongst them his wife, Carpenter and Symonds), were central to his argument. They were carefully selected (and in some cases doctored) to put them in the most favourable light possible. Just as earlier case-histories, in Krafft-Ebing's work for instance, were biased towards sickness, so Ellis's were biased towards health. They illustrated the major part of his argument: the strength of homosexual feeling; its ineradicability despite moral repression; its wide distribution (interestingly the working-class 'inverts' cited seemed to accept their homosexuality more easily than those from the professional class); its lack of pathological forms; the absence of effeminacy, and the variety of sexual expression. The great majority of people cited found themselves fully able to accept their inversion. Those who did not nevertheless emerged as towers of moral strength.

If homosexuality was not a medical problem, then there was no necessity for a 'cure'. Ellis briefly discussed various methods of 'cure' – particularly hypnotism and psychoanalysis – and found them wanting. The various disorders often associated with homosexuality, he felt, were more often associated with society's attitudes than with the sexual orientation itself.[33] And this pointed to the necessity of changing the law. The arguments he put forward (influenced in the first place by J.A.Symonds's essays) questioned whether the law had a right to intervene in private behaviour; questioned the effectiveness of the law in catching homosexuals, or in stopping homosexual behaviour; recognised the encouragement the law gave to blackmail; and pointed to the general absurdity of a law which made 'gross indecency' (usually mutual masturbation between men) illegal while masturbation itself was not a penal offence. He concluded that the law should only concern itself with preventing violence and protecting the young and public order: 'Whatever laws are laid down beyond this must be left to the individuals themselves, to the moralists, and to social opinion.'[34]

These were exactly the arguments put forward some 60 years later in the liberal campaign to change the law relating to homosexuality in England and Wales in the wake of the Wolfenden Report. The whole force of *Sexual Inversion*, its tempered tone, its often muted evidence, was directed to this end.

The type of case Ellis argued has had a long history among reformers. Three elements have been central: firstly, the argument that homosexuality is characteristic of a fixed minority, and is incurable: secondly, that reforming efforts should be directed towards changing the law so that this minority may live in peace; thirdly, the belief that such reform would only come about by a long period of public education. Few people until very recently argued for more than this. Indeed, even the abolition of penalties against homosexuality in Russia after the Bolshevik Revolution did not go beyond this (the direct influence there being the similar work of Magnus Hirschfeld).

But though liberal sexual ideology 'tolerates' homosexuality it always begins with the assumption that homosexual behaviour has to be explained as a deviation from a norm of sexual behaviour. What has to be tolerated in this view is an 'abnormality', however gently this is stated. Ellis, despite his efforts to find a relatively neutral form of words, was no exception to this. He stressed the impossibility of getting 'social opinion' to accept homosexuality and found it difficult therefore to advise a reluctant homosexual to 'set himself in violent opposition' to his society. There was, in his view, a need for a reluctant acquiescence in the moral views of society, and much the best result for the homosexual would be attained:

When, while retaining his own ideas, or inner instincts, he resolves to forgo alike the attempt to become normal and the attempt to secure the grosser gratification of his abnormal desires.[35]

Ellis's scepticism about the possibility of radical changes in attitudes stemmed from deeper roots than simple caution. Fundamentally, he was trapped within the conservatism that his biological theories dictated.

His attitude to lesbianism is particularly relevant here. He claimed that his work gave special attention to female homosexuality, and by comparison with his predecessors this might well be the case. There is, for instance, a complete dearth of references to lesbianism in Krafft-Ebing's *Psychopathia Sexualis*. Ellis was, as a matter of course, as prepared to publicly defend the rights of lesbians as he was of male homosexuals. His wife, Edith Ellis, was lesbian, a fact which became quite well known. A lecture tour of the USA by Edith had reached the headlines of the Chicago press when she defended lesbian relations. In the 1920s Ellis defended Radclyffe Hall's lesbian novel, *The Well of Loneliness*, and contributed a preface to it. He stated that his *Sexual Inversion* had, from its first edition, given special attention to lesbianism. Nevertheless, only one chapter of *Sexual Inversion* is entirely concerned with lesbianism and only six case-histories are properly described. References to it in later volumes of his *Studies* are similarly spare. Two immediate explanations occur. Firstly, there was possibly an element of personal embarrassment, given Edith's own lesbianism. Secondly, there was a great absence of easily obtainable information. There was no visible sub-culture in Britain for lesbians until later in this century, unlike the situation for male homosexuals. And lesbianism was not illegal – largely because it was scarcely recognised – so there were few spectacular court cases and no compelling reason for a political campaign on the question. There is, however, a curiosity in Ellis's approach. While he went to considerable lengths to stress that male homosexuals were *not* effeminate, he stresses that lesbians *were* inclined to be masculine. He believed the use of the dildo was common, and played down the importance of clitoral sexuality.[36]

Beyond this was his conviction that 'masculinity' and 'femininity' were qualities which were based on deep biological differences. In this view, male sexuality was basically active; female was essentially passive and responsive to the male's. If this was the case lesbianism, which asserts the autonomy of female sexuality, could only be explained by Ellis as a deeply rooted element of masculinity in the woman. As a result Ellis did not seem able to challenge existing stereotypes of lesbian behaviour.

Today, it is increasingly recognised that the sexual organs a person is born with do not in themselves pre-determine either sexual behaviour or social roles. These are learnt, in the family and in society at large. This concept offers a fundamental challenge to theories which rely solely on biological concepts of behaviour.

Ellis, in fact, flirted with certain ideas which re-stated an original bisexual constitution in every individual. As an idea, it dated back to ancient Greece, and perhaps earlier, but it was just at this period, in the late nineteenth and early twentieth centuries, that the notion became the subject of scientific investigation. European writers like Wilhelm Fleiss, Otto Weininger and Freud made it central parts of their theories. It is potentially radical because it does open up the possibility that roles are socially moulded rather than dictated by nature.

Ellis was at one with these writers in recognising that both sexes had elements of intersexuality, recessive characteristics of the opposite sex. But he fundamentally disagreed with Freud over how this should be interpreted. He felt that Freud's theory of the Oedipus complex suggested that bisexuality ought to be regarded as the basic state, so that homosexuality arose through the suppression of the heterosexual element. This opened up the possibility of similarly regarding heterosexuality as the product of the suppression of homosexual elements. Ellis recognised the dangers of this for his concept of the congenital basis of sexual behaviour:

If a man becomes attracted to his own sex simply because the fact or image of such attraction is brought before him, then we are bound to believe that a man becomes attracted to the opposite sex only because the fact or image of such attraction is brought before him. Such a theory is unworkable.[37]

If he were to accept Freud's views then he would have to accept that the 'most fundamental' human instinct could equally well be adapted to 'sterility' as to propagation of the race. Such a view, Ellis believed, would not fit into any 'rational biological scheme'.

Ellis followed Magnus Hirschfeld in emphasising the role of

congenital influences. The discovery at the beginning of this century of the importance of hormones in determining male/female characteristics provided an apparently 'scientific' basis for an explanation. Ellis believed that each child was born with an equal number of sex determining factors of either sex. Sexual difference emerged when one set of these elements asserted themselves over the other in the course of development, so that homosexuality arose because of an imbalance of the 'correct' elements. For Ellis, then, sexual differences were based on physiological differences which emerged more or less spontaneously, being rooted in the individual heredity.

Ellis regarded this disagreement with Freud as of central importance, and it coloured their relationship. Freud, in later debates with Hirschfeld's followers in Germany, was to concede in the 1920s that certain elements of homosexuality might be congenital, and Ellis, as we have seen, conceded the possibility of environmental influences. But at stake was the larger issue of the extent to which external influences could influence emotional and sexual patterns. Freud's theories at least left open the possibility that historical changes might alter sexual behaviour and sexual roles. Ellis, wedded to biological theories, remained more sceptical.

Ellis's work on homosexuality was not strikingly original in method or content. *Sexual Inversion* is essentially a work of synthesis, much influenced by Hirschfeld's researches, particularly on the importance of hormones, and on transvestism. Moreover, in comparison with later volumes of his *Studies* it is thinner, in detail and vigour, a fact underlined by his later revision of the first editions. But its form is the central fact about it: Ellis was arguing a case which history has made not less but more pressing. This must be noted at the same time as we criticise its conceptual inadequacies.

### The Laws of Nature

There were two, ultimately contradictory, elements in Ellis's work. Firstly, he attempted to stress the value and importance of sex in people's lives and the pleasure that could be got from it. From James Hinton he had learnt the dynamic nature of sexuality, influencing many varied aspects of a person's behaviour. Like Freud he was a pioneer in stressing the existence of childhood sexuality, though he felt that Freud exaggerated its closeness to adult sex. And, again with Freud, he traced the sexual origins of many apparently disparate phenomena, such as hysteria. Although Ellis was unable to accept the revolutionary implications of many of Freud's bolder theories, believing he was too sweeping in his generalisations, seeing as universal what was culturally specific, he shared with him a common aim – to widen the acceptable definitions of sexuality – and as a result, despite their ambiguous intellectual dialogue, their work is to a large extent complementary.

To Ellis's mind sexuality was not something to be regarded with horror. It was a powerful force which suffused and enhanced the whole of life. 'Auto-erotism', which formed the subject of the second volume of his *Studies* was, Ellis believed, its prime symptom.

'Auto-erotism', a term Ellis coined, he defined as the sexual energy of a person automatically generated throughout life, and manifesting itself without any definite external stimulation. Its typical manifestation was orgasm during sleep and involuntary emissions, though it also included erotic daydreams, narcissism and hysteria. In opposition to conventional restrictiveness, Ellis felt it wiser to recognise the inevitability of these sexual manifestations and their relative harmlessness. He recommended the avoidance of both excessive indulgence and of excessive horror.

Ellis stressed what most people had always recognised in practice, that sex could be enjoyed, and did not just serve the utilitarian function of procreation. So just as Ellis gave cautious approval to the most public form of non-utilitarian sex – homosexuality – so he did to the most private – masturbation – which had been subject to ferocious taboos in the nineteenth century, and to which had been ascribed all sorts of physical and mental enfeeblement. He demonstrated that there was no evidence linking masturbation with any serious mental or physical disorder, and he pointed to its enormous prevalence. Even more striking was his view that it was particularly prevalent – indeed even more common – amongst women than men.

Ellis was not quite able to bring himself to give an absolute carte-blanche to masturbation. Like Freud who believed it well into the 1920s, Ellis felt that there were harmful side effects. He could not entirely free himself of the myth that sex was a drain on a person's productive energies. Moreover, he felt that excessive masturbation in youth might leave a person incapable of associating sexuality with love. But at least he attempted to remove the spurious medical gloss from it.[38]

In the same way he examined other non-reproductive forms of sex and sex-related behaviour, particularly in a supplementary volume of his *Studies*, published in 1927. Coprophilia, undinism, sadism and masochism, frotage, kleptomania, narcissism, necrophilia and many others: all were examined with dispassionate interest, with a wealth of cross-cultural evidence detailing their incidence. In the supplementary volume he also examined at length the nature of transvestism, or cross dressing, developing the brief references in *Sexual Inversion*.[39] He followed Hirschfeld in seeing it as a largely heterosexual phenomenon, only remotely connected to homosexuality, and quite separate in origin. With his passion as a 'naturalist' Ellis refused to either condone or condemn: these things existed, and they were only harmful when another individual was hurt. In the relationship of the male and female, Ellis argued, all varieties of sexual activities were allowable. He showed that other cultures had sanctioned various forms of coitus, and that fellatio, cunnilingus, buggery, all played a useful preliminary role in sexual behaviour. Typically, however, Ellis saw these only as aspects of sexual foreplay, not activities valid in themselves. They became 'abnormal', he believed, when they substituted themselves for the 'real aims of sexuality' – the act by which the race is propagated.[40]

This brings us to the second element of Ellis's attitudes. For he sought to relate all the so-called sexual 'anomalies' to a single process, rooted in the biological make-up of men and women. And in so doing, his work increasingly sought to confirm, rather than challenge, the conventional interpretations of male and female sexual roles.

The process which gave coherence to sexuality Ellis called 'courtship'. Courtship was rooted in the most primitive acts of the animal world, the sexual conquest of the female of the species by the male. It was the process in which sexual excitement was built up in the partners, arousing the mechanisms which bring about orgasm (Ellis called them 'tumescence' and 'detumescence'). All the so-called 'perversions' were actually distortions, Ellis believed, of this activity.[41] So for instance, sadism was just an exaggeration of the pain causing inherent in the sexual act, while transvestism ('sexo-aesthetic inversion') was a product of an exaggerated identification with the object of one's sexual attraction. In other words, Ellis was suggesting a 'continuum' between 'normal' and 'abnormal' phenomena, and this idea has been of major importance in modern works on sexual theory (e.g. the work of Alfred Kinsey). But the essential element in 'courtship' for Ellis was the *male* wooing the *female* for the sake of procreation, and in this formulation Ellis was already undermining his acceptance of 'anomalies'. For the two central strands of conventional attitudes remained: firstly, that the male was the initiator of sex, and the woman was receptive; second, that the chief justification of sexual activity was procreation, the act of perpetuating 'the race'. These came together in his attitude to women and their role.

Ellis's work belonged to a tradition which expected significant changes for women to come about only through enlarging the sphere in which their sex-determined characteristics could flourish. And in some ways this did involve an advance in the supposedly 'scientific' definition of womanhood. Ellis rejected for example that element of nineteenth-century ideology which attempted to deny female sexuality altogether. William Acton, whom Ellis took to be the typical representative of the Victorian 'double standard', presented an image of male sexuality as forceful, direct and uncontrollable, while female sexuality was not recognised as existing, 'a vile aspersion'.[42] Common sense, let alone theory, told Ellis that this was little more than a myth, one he believed peculiar to the nineteenth century, and to a few western countries (Britain, Germany, Italy). Ellis believed that a woman had a right to have her sexuality satisfied and typically he argued that there was a biological justification for a woman enjoying sex: sexual excitement in women was essential to combat sterility. Moreover, he recognised that mutual sexual satisfaction was not automatic; it was a technique, which could be learned and by the male at that.[43] Female indifference or frigidity lay not in the woman but often in the male's inadequacies.

But on the other hand Ellis had very fixed concepts of male and female sexuality. He saw the male's as 'open and aggressive', and to his mind this was so obvious that a special investigation of it was unnecessary. It was woman's sexuality that was problematical, because through it the race was propagated.[44] A large part of Ellis's work is thus concerned with female sexuality; it is both a landmark in the study of sexuality, and an indication of how persistent sexual stereotypes were.

He defined a woman's sexuality as essentially secondary, responsive to that of a man. The male must generally take the initiative in sexual matters. His role in courting the female is, through displaying his energy (which Ellis saw as the characteristic of men) and skill, to capture the female and arouse her to an emotional condition by which she surrenders sexually to him. 'The female responds to the stimulation of the male at the right moment just as the tree responds to the stimulation of the warmest days in spring.'

He believed that the sex life of the woman was largely conditioned by the sex life of the man, so that while a youth spontaneously becomes a man, the woman 'must be kissed into a woman'. The woman attracts by her beauty, while the man attracts by his strength, physical or mental.[45]

Ellis detected a particular characteristic of woman called 'modesty', which was so prevalent that it amounted to almost the chief secondary characteristic of woman. It was the element of female refusal, which safeguarded her, and at the same time aroused the male. The apparent passivity of the female was, Ellis believed, essential to the full success of courtship. He made it clear that attitudes to modesty have changed throughout history. He cites the Turkish prostitutes who were more concerned with covering their faces than their organs, and the Tahitians seen by Captain Cook who did not mind copulating in public but would never dine together. But though the forms of modesty might change, the fact of it was a characteristic part of femininity.[46]

Ellis is clearly reading into 'nature' the social forms of masculine and feminine behaviour that he observed around him: the male is active, initiatory; the female passive, responsive. He is surrendering to the positivist delusion of confusing the surface appearance of things for their real potentiality. Both the existence of lesbianism and of female masturbation, which he acknowledged, demonstrate the actual autonomy of female sexuality. Any 'passivity' that may be observed is more the product of social conditioning than of 'nature'. On the basis of his ahistorical description, however, Ellis builds his theory of the different social roles that men and women should play.

In his book *Man and Woman* (first published in 1893, and among the most frequently republished of his books) Ellis examines what he called the secondary and tertiary characteristics of men and women. His conclusion is that there is in nature a 'cosmic conservatism', a natural harmony, which had become: 'as nearly perfect as possible, and every inaptitude is compensated by some compensatory aptitude'.

For a just society, therefore, each sex must follow 'the laws of its own nature'. For Ellis the fundamental truth of natural life was that the two sexes were separately defined in evolution only as a method of favouring reproduction, and this could only partially be over-ridden. Nature therefore sanctified the social roles that men and women inhabited: 'woman breeds and tends; man provides; it remains so even when the spheres tend to overlap'.[47]

There was Ellis believed an organic basis for the separate social spheres. For associated with the woman's *biological* capacity to produce children were fundamental 'feminine' characteristics: not only modesty, but affectability, sympathy, maternal instincts, devotion, emotional receptivity. These were essential to woman's sphere. And accompanying these advantages were compensating disadvantages: biological barriers to women performing satisfactorily in competition with men in their sphere. Amongst these were the biological imperatives of motherhood, and the debilitating effects of menstruation.[48]

Nature therefore defined a woman's true sphere as motherhood, the supreme position which life had to offer. In a particularly devastating phrase Ellis wrote that women's brains are 'in a certain sense ... in their wombs', and when he speaks of pregnancy as a woman's destiny his language becomes extraordinarily elevated: the woman is 'lifted above the level of ordinary humanity to become the casket of an inestimable jewel'.

While the male's task as defined by nature is to 'forage abroad' and 'stand on guard' in the antechamber of the family, the female's is to care for the children and the husband.[49]

In his *Origins of the Family* Engels had argued that the subordination of women was a result of the historical developments which gave economic dominance to men through the development of private property. Even in the working-class family, which was propertyless, the husband because of his direct involvement in social production, had economic dominance over the wife: in the working-class family, Engels wrote, the man was the bourgeois. Engels concluded that the precondition for women's equality with man was her economic liberation through direct involvement in social labour, which would only be fully achieved in a socialist society. Only on the basis of economic equality could individual sex-love between the woman and the man flourish, the woman be released from her enslavement in the house, and child care and housework be socialised.

Though Ellis never appears to mention Engels' work (it was not published in English until the early twentieth century) he must have been familiar with the main lines of its arguments. He had, in the 1880s, reviewed August Bebel's book on *Women and Socialism* and he himself argued that morality had hitherto been based on private property, as particularly revealed in the workings of the English divorce laws, where 'the infidelity of the wife was a serious crime against property'.[50] But against Engel's advocacy of economic equality based on female integration into the work force, Ellis argued for a *moral* equality based on the separation of roles.

Ellis increasingly believed that the women's movement had gone in the wrong direction in demanding for women equal opportunity with men in industry and the professions (particularly the latter: it was mainly middle-class women who made the demand). By 1912 he was highly critical of the tactics and aims of the suffragettes of the Women's Social and Political Union (WSPU). Although he recognised the importance of the vote, and the crucial role the WSPU had played in energising the women's movement, he criticised them for sectarianism, narrowness of aim, increased conventionality and a tendency to 'morbid emotionalism'.[51] Many feminists tended to agree with him that law reform was not enough. Emma Goldman, for one, shared many of his complaints and was influenced by his ideas. As an alternative Ellis believed that feminists should follow the German movement in stressing the question of motherhood.

Ellis's views were deeply influenced at this time by the work of the Swedish feminist, Ellen Key, whose works, *The Century of the Child, The Women's Movement* and *Love and Marriage*, he helped to introduce to an English-speaking public. She argued essentially that women did need free scope for their activities, so that in this sense early feminist aspirations were justified. But the real need was not to wrest away from men tasks that men might be better able to fulfil, but for women to play their part in that field of creative life which was peculiarly their own. As a result, Ellen Key believed that the highest human unit was 'triune': father, mother, and child, with marriage becoming the central point of life.[52]

This involved the social recognition and elevation of motherhood and Ellis took up this point. At present, he believed, motherhood was without dignity: the vitality of mothers was crushed; there was widespread ignorance about sexuality and childbirth; the care and protection of the pregnant woman and the young child was ignored. To combat this the mother must become the dominant parent – he assigned her, for instance, the central role in sex education – and must be fully trained for her role. He even appears to approve of Ellen Key's notion that each woman should do a year's compulsory service in housekeeping.[53] He argued, therefore, for a confirmation of the woman's traditional sphere, with state help to make it function more efficiently.

The radical emphasis of the modern women's liberation movement has been the challenge to the identification of womanhood with housekeeping and child-rearing, which serves not the interest of women but the sexual division of labour under capitalism. Ellis worked within the existing preconceptions and argued that women should withdraw from social labour. This would be easier, he stated, for working-class women than for professional. The fact that working-class women usually had to work to maintain a minimum standard of life seems to have escaped him. But to compensate Ellis believed that the state must take a greater part in aiding and regulating motherhood.

Ellis saw in the liberal reforms of the years before 1914 evidence of the growing recognition of the importance of motherhood and the care of the child. The setting up of child guidance clinics, school meals, schemes for the 'endowment of motherhood', the compulsory registration of births, were in fact important steps forward, and did help to improve the lot of working-class mothers. But if they are just seen as well-intentioned liberal reforms their true significance is lost. The new emphasis on the social role of motherhood must be placed in a wider context. The Boer War (1898–1902) had demonstrated the appalling physical condition of working-class recruits into the British army. The 1904 report of an inter-departmental committee on physical conditions headed by General Maurice had caused a great furore in the ruling class, and a conviction that the stock of the imperial race was endangered. As Ellis put it: 'The State needs healthy men and women, and by any negligence in attending to this need it . . . dangerously impairs its efficiency in the world.'

Healthy mothers and children were needed to breed an imperial race capable of competing in the new era of imperialist rivalries. And this was the rationale behind the 'national efficiency' campaigns launched by a motley bunch of right-wing Tories, Liberals and Fabians in the aftermath of the Boer War. Ellis saw the liberal reforms, and particularly the 1908 Notification of Births Act, as the 'national inauguration of a scheme for the betterment of the race', and as a triumph for 'national efficiency'. Many of these reforms Ellis had in fact anticipated in a short book entitled *The Nationalisation of Health* published in 1892.

As one would expect, military metaphors abounded at this period. Ellis quotes with approval Ellen Key's phrase that:

as a general rule the woman who refuses motherhood in order to serve humanity, is like a soldier who prepares himself on the eve of battle for the forthcoming struggle by opening his veins.[54]

The theme of social betterment becomes increasingly dominant in Ellis's work. He advocated that every *healthy* woman should at least once in her life exercise her supreme function in the interests of the race. Moreover, in opposition to the socialist tradition which theoretically at least favoured the socialisation of housework and child rearing, he believed that the rearing of the child would best be served by each mother being responsible for the individual upbringing of the child. This was in keeping, as he saw it, both with the aptitudes of the mother, and the best interests of healthy childhood.

Ellis's growing concern with 'the future of the race' inevitably brought him into sympathy with the eugenics movement. This movement had a considerable impact in the early decades of the century, and it provided Ellis with an ideology which offered a new outlook on social improvements. If, as he argued, the reproduction of the species was the supreme aim of life, then it was here that social reform should concentrate.

Eugenics was a theory of improving the human stock by selective breeding. Essentially utopian in outlook, it believed that the identification of inborn characteristics would make possible the elimination of the weakly and the unfit. Ellis defined it as:

The scientific study of all the agencies by which the human race may be improved, and the effort to give practical effect to those agencies by conscious and deliberate action in favour of better breeding.[55]

In its origins in the late nineteenth century, eugenics theories had been seized on by reformers of a pre-marxist outlook who saw in its ideas a useful supplement to social reform. But in its emphasis on innate characteristics as opposed to environmental influences it fitted in more usefully with the ideas of conservatives opposed to social change. In England the chief theorist was Francis Galton whose general outlook was arch-conservative. His work became generally known from about 1905–6, in the wake of the panic over 'racial suicide' and he was the inspirer of the Eugenics Education Society founded in 1908.

Ellis's interest was of longstanding. He mentioned Galton's work in his essay on 'Women and Socialism' as early as 1884, and had even criticised Galton for what he called his timidity over the 'central problem', that of control of population.[56] From the early 1900s, however, it became the key element of continuity in his sexual studies. His book *Sex in Relation to Society* which sums up his *Studies*, climaxes on two themes: 'The Art of Love' and the 'Science of Procreation'. He makes it clear that they must be interdependent, one the condition of the other.

Ellis believed that 'eugenics' was the ultimate stage of the movement for social reform. Hitherto, the social reform movement had concentrated on improving the environment. This was important, but not enough. It was now necessary to purify 'the stream of life' at its source, and to concentrate on the 'point of procreation'.[57] To his mind eugenics represented the highest point which social reform had reached.

The supreme danger of all eugenics arguments is that they are filtered through the ruling class: it is they who decide whether the population is too large or small, which part of it is superior or inferior, which people have to limit their procreation. And inevitably, it was linked with ideas of racial superiority. Much of the debate in the pre-First World War period was over the declining birth rate and over whether it was the 'best class' which was declining most rapidly. The 'best class' in this terminology was the upper class and even Ellis, who regarded such questions as 'hazardous', felt constrained to accept that it was generally so. In his book, *A Study of British Genius*, he noted that the vast majority of the population (the working-class and women) produced the least amount of genius, and concluded that 'genius' revealed a high degree of heredity. With regard to the more mundane level of life, the criterion which Ellis used was 'fitness' – mental or physical. It followed that generally the least fit were those from lower-class families where conditions and facilities were bad. The question of improving the conditions and opportunities of life thus became inextricably involved with questions of class and of control of reproduction, and the ideals of socialism became confused with the mechanisms of state control.

Ellis's confusions were common in the socialist movement. Eugenics in some ways rushed in to fill the gap in socialist theories over sexual matters so that: 'particularly on the question of racial and ethnic differences, the left did not offer an especially enlightened leadership'.[58]

Karl Pearson, who was Galton's closest disciple, and certainly called himself a socialist at that period, wrote in 1885: 'If child-bearing women must be intellectually handicapped, then the penalty to be paid for race predominance is the subjection of women.'

The work of Galton and Pearson greatly influenced other socialists. H.G.Wells, who was present at an exposition of eugenics by Galton, had a rush of blood to the head and advocated the 'sterilisation of failures', while Sidney Webb felt that unless the decline in the birth rate was arrested the nation would fall to the Irish and the Jews.[59]

These writers were closer to social imperialism than to revolutionary socialism. But even the more radical writers succumbed. Eden Paul, a member of the ILP and later a member of the Communist Party, worried over eugenics before 1914, and wrote: 'Unless the socialist is a eugenicist as well, the socialist state will speedily perish from racial degradation.'[60]

Eden Paul believed that the ability to earn a minimum wage must be the condition of the right to become a parent. Behind this was the conviction, even amongst socialists, that distinction could be made between the 'deserving' and the 'undeserving' poor.

One of the major rationales of 'neo-Malthusian' ideas was that, by limiting the growth of the population of the unfit poor, they would help solve the problem of chronic unemployment which seemed to many a product of nature rather than of capitalism. Marx had long ago punctured the bubble of Malthusian myths but they survived, even among socialists despairing of rapid social change. Moreover, such was the predominance of social-Darwinist ideas that few people would have questioned, before the racialist terrors of the 1920s and 1930s, that some people were innately better endowed than others.

Many of the early proponents of eugenics equated it with a new religion. Galton called for a 'Jehad' – a Holy War to be declared on the survival of ancient dysgenic customs, and urged that eugenics – 'a virile creed' – should become a 'religious tenet' of the future. In the same fashion Ellen Key believed that men and women would eventually devote the same religious fervour to propagating the race as Christians devoted to the salvation of souls.[61]

Ellis on the other hand adopted a slightly more measured position. He rejected what he called eugenic fanaticism, and he denied that it was eugenicist to speak of one race being better than another. He preferred, he said, to speak of the 'human race', and to speak of 'quality' of person rather than 'quantity'. Moreover, he believed that knowledge was not yet sufficient to justify a *positive* eugenics: breeding of the best. It was only possible to develop a *negative* eugenics, designed to eliminate the unfit, by which he seems to have meant the 'feeble-minded'. And he rejected compulsion, so though he favoured health tests before marriage, the encouragement of the best classes to marry, and the sterilisation of the unfit, he believed that this would only come about through education, not direction. In accord, therefore, with the whole trend of his work, he believed the first necessity was to create a new enthusiasm for health and moral awareness in matters relating to reproduction.

Ellis believed that it was women who should be the focus for the education. And he saw two 'practical' ways in which eugenics ideas would spread; through the development of a 'sense of sexual responsibility' in men and women; and through the development of effective contraception (including abortion, of which he was a pioneer advocate). In practice both involved the 'autonomous authority' of women: 'The State has no more right than the individual to ravish a woman against her will.'[62] Nevertheless, of course, the whole point of Ellis's arguments was to confirm women in their exclusive child-bearing role. Ellis recognised the necessity of women controlling their own sexuality but this was theoretically and practically hampered by a prior commitment to the sort of social role women should perform.

A subtle change in terminology reveals the dangers. Margaret Sanger, the American feminist had coined the phrase 'birth control', and this suggested the liberating possibilities in the development of contraception. The name of Marie Stopes's society which campaigned for birth control after the First World War added another element: Society for Constructive Birth Control and *Racial Progress*. By the 1930s the emphasis had shifted again: to 'population control' and 'family planning'. The radical possibilities of contraception depended then, as now, on the existence of a radical women's movement which recognised the central importance of women regulating their own fertility. The disappearance of such a women's movement in the 1920s and '30s subordinated the campaigns for birth control to the demands of class society and the ideology of 'stable middle-class families'. In practice in the bourgeois family, whatever the ideology of equality between the partners, the female is constrained by her procreative function and domestic duties and subordinated to the economic and social power of the husband. The idea of reproductive self-determination had become swamped in the social control of contraception. Ellis, who continued to assert the primacy of eugenics into the 1930s, was himself chiefly concerned with the problem of 'control' rather than of a woman's right of free choice.[63]

One example of this was a distinct hardening of Ellis's attitude to the role of the family. In his early writings, Ellis emerged as a critic of the Victorian family and marriage system. The legal system of monogamy, he argued, was a product of class society, and the development of private property. He likened contemporary marriage to prostitution, in that it subordinated the wife to the authority and whim of the man. In some ways, he felt, the prostitute was better off: more rapes had occurred in marriage than outside it. He therefore favoured reform of marriage, and both in his life and in his early work he advocated what he (and Edith Ellis) called a 'companionate', or ethical union of two people in which the equal rights of both partners would be respected. His own marriage strove to follow this model. He and Edith lived apart for large parts of the year, attempted to enjoy their separate incomes, and both had emotional and sexual entanglements outside the marriage, while remaining emotionally loyal and open with one another. Ellis argued strongly that the state had the right to intervene in marriage laws only where children were involved in order to safeguard the child. But of course this was the crux. For in his social ideas the family came to assume an increasing importance, as he became more deeply involved in eugenics. And as was typical in his work he accepted the view that monogamy was 'natural', rooted in the biology of men and women. By the 1930s the emphasis on the importance of marriage in cementing a monogamous union had become more pronounced. In his textbook, *Psychology of Sex*, first published in 1933, the emphasis on the need for love between partners is still clear. But now he cautiously advises against rash marriages, or cross-cultural or cross-religious matches, because of the danger of incompatibility. And he stresses the importance of medical examinations, and of mutual knowledge of each other's anatomy and physiology as well as feelings, for 'Marriage is much more than a sexual relationship.'[64]

It was, in fact, in his eyes, the key to social policy, for it was through the family that the future of the human race could be ensured. As in much else of his work Ellis's ideas prefigured many of the arguments which have become the ideological glue of the welfare state. Ellis's views on marriage and motherhood found their realisation in the idea of family allowances, the state supporting the family in the interests of healthy childhood and social stability. And his advocacy of reformed marriages, with equal rights for both partners, finds its outcome today in ideas of the 'Symmetrical Family'.[65] By an apparent paradox, the writer who had first achieved notoriety as an advocate of sexual freedom, ended his career as the liberal advocate of a reformed family, where social roles are cemented rather than questioned.

## Middle Ways

Ellis once advised Margaret Sanger to follow a middle road in challenging authority. It was a middle road that Ellis travelled in his advocacy of sex reform, and as a result many of his views have now become commonplace. Unlike his near contemporary Sigmund Freud, he left behind no clear theoretical heritage, no school of devoted followers, no sustained effort to found a new science of sexology as Freud attempted to found a science of psychoanalysis. The content of Ellis's major work, *Studies in the Psychology of Sex*, now seems empirically dated and theoretically weak compared to the imaginative flights of a Freud.

Nevertheless, an analysis of Ellis's work does reveal a great deal about the nature, strengths and weaknesses of the pathmakers in sexual frankness. For he attempted to sum up and give coherence to the various reforming attitudes that were in the air. In his writings we can see the effort needed to break out of the Victorian taboos; and the scars that the struggle left behind.

In the first place it is important to recognise Ellis's role as an *ideologist*. The purpose of his works was to change attitudes and to create a new view of the role of sex in individual lives and in society. He set out to rationalise sexual theory, and in doing so helped lay down the foundations of a 'liberal' ideology of sex. The essence of this was a greater toleration of sexual variations; a desire to relax the rigid moral code; and an emphasis on the 'joys of sex'. Its weakness was its inability to ask *why* societies have continued to control sexuality and persecute sexual minorities throughout the ages; and as a result its eventual absorption into capitalist value structures.

Secondly, and perhaps his most real and lasting achievement, he was a pioneer in bringing together and categorising information on the different types of sexual experience. Even this, to us apparently elementary task, shocked his contemporaries. It was, however, an essential preliminary to any rational study of sexuality. From it stemmed two central strands in his approach: the acceptance of the (now largely discredited) view of the biological roots of sexual variations – particularly homosexuality; and the use of evidence from other cultures to underline his argument that morals were not unchanging or unchangeable, but were in constant evolution. The *Studies* are a pot-pourri of details about the enormous variety of sexual experiences through different times and climes.

Thirdly, he recognised that the question of the social roles of the two sexes was of paramount importance in the new century, particularly because of the influence of the women's movement. He therefore attempted to suggest guidelines for more humane and equal sexual and social relations and behaviour. The particular form these guidelines took now seem among the most reactionary aspects of his work – particularly his view of woman's role – and reveal clearly the ways in which he was trapped within the stereotyped images that he inherited. And yet, for a long period, his preoccupations were shared by all progressive tendencies, including revolutionary socialists. Marxism in its great period rarely ventured to work out a materialist theory of sexuality, but relied on the most advanced bourgeois theories. This left a yawning gap in socialist notions of sexuality which has continued to this day, and which has allowed all sorts of backward ideas to rush in.

But to grasp fully Ellis's impact we must also look at the way he was viewed by his contemporaries. Margaret Sanger spoke of the tremendous sense of excitement she felt when she first encountered Ellis, and this seems to have been a common response. Conservative leaders of the women's movement shunned his overt support in case his reputation damaged the cause, while radicals such as Stella Browne, Emma Goldman and Margaret Sanger saw him as a giant who:

beyond any other person, has been able to clarify the question of sex and free it from the smudginess connected with it from the beginning of Christianity, raise it from the dark cellar, set it on a higher plain.[66]

Ellis provided a rationale for sex reform which, inadequate as it now appears, was a major achievement for his time. It is this which justifies placing Ellis as one of the pioneer sexual enlighteners of the twentieth century.

### References

**1.** Margaret Sanger is quoted in Arthur Calder-Marshall, *Havelock Ellis*, London, Rupert Hart-Davis 1959, p.154. Other comments come from Samuel Hynes, *The Edwardian Turn of Mind*, Princeton University Press 1968, p.171, p.149; E.H.Brecher, *The Sex Researchers*, London, Andre Deutsch 1971 and Paul A.Robinson, 'Havelock Ellis and Modern Sexual Theory' in *Salamagundi*, No. 21, Winter 1973. This is the best modern discussion of Ellis's sexual ideas. It is the basis for the section on Ellis in Paul Robinson, *The Modernisation of Sex*, London, Elek 1976. For works on his life, see Calder-Marshall's biography; and Isaac Goldberg, *Havelock Ellis*, London, Constable 1926: Ellis's autobiography, *My Life*, London, Heinemann 1940, is very revealing. The biographical details in this article come from these works.

**2.** S.Hynes, *op. cit.*, p.132.

**3.** Havelock Ellis, *The Dance of Life*, London, Constable 1923, p.204.

**4.** Ellis, *My Life*, 1967 ed, pp.130–131. For further details of Ellis's ideas, see Robert Sprich, 'The World as Beauty', *Man and Society*, No. 14, Winter 1973–74.

**5.** Ellis, *The New Spirit*, London, G. Bell & Sons 1889, pp.6,9,13.

**6.** Goldberg, *op. cit.*, p.99.

**7.** See W.H.G.Armytage, *Heavens Below. Utopian Experiments in England, 1560–1960*, London, Routledge & Kegan Paul 1961, pp.331ff.

**8.** G.B.Shaw, *Fabian Tract* No. 41, quoted in Calder-Marshall, *op. cit.*, p.87.

**9.** Quoted in Armytage, *op. cit.*, p.332.

**10.** H. Ellis, *The Task of Social Hygiene*, London, Constable 1912, p.389.

**11.** Armytage, *op. cit.*, p.332.

**12.** See, for example, Ellis, 'Women and Socialism', *Today*, vol. 2, July–December 1884, p.363.

**13.** Ellis, *The New Spirit*, p.9.

**14.** Ellis, *The New Spirit*, 4th ed, London, Constable 1926, p.viii. He wrote in the General Preface to the 1st edition of *Sexual Inversion*, p.v: 'As a youth, I had hoped to settle problems for those who came after: now I am quite content if I do little more than state them.' He cites the question of sex – to which he significantly adds 'the racial question' – as the outstanding problem of the day in this same preface, p.x.

**15.** See Brecher, *The Sex Researchers*, for details.

**16.** Dr Elizabeth Blackwell, *The Human Element in Sex*, London, J. and A. Churchill 1884, p.32.

**17.** See R.Krafft-Ebing, *Psychopathia Sexualis*, trans. of 7th ed, London, F.A.Davis & Co. 1892, pp.288–9. Krafft-Ebing's work was to have a long history and influence. It was still the basic sex manual for the girls in Mary McCarthy's novel *The Group*, set in the 1930s.

**18.** Ellis, *Sexual Inversion*, 1897 ed, p.xix. *Sexual Inversion* was later republished in a fuller and revised form as vol. 2, part 2, of *Studies in the Psychology of Sex*, New York, Random House 1936, 4 vols. All references, except when otherwise stated, are to this final edition of the *Studies*. More details regarding nineteenth-century attitudes can be found in Jeffrey Weeks '"Sins and Diseases": Some notes on homosexuality in the ninteenth century'. *History Workshop Journal*, No. 1, Spring 1976.

**19.** See Ellis, *The New Spirit*; see also *My Life*, p.263.

**20.** See H.M.Scheuller and R.L.Peters (eds), *The Letters of John Addington Symonds*, vol. III, 1885–93, Detroit, 1969. L.1791, 6 May 1890; L.1984 and L.1996, June–July 1895. For biographical details see Phyllis Grosskurth, *John Addington Symonds*, London, Constable 1964.

**21.** Ellis to Carpenter, 17 December 1892. (Letter in Edward Carpenter Collection, Sheffield City Libraries.)

**22.** For Symonds's comment see *Letters*, L.1996, p.710. Tuke was probably so hostile because his own son, a minor artist, was himself notoriously homosexual.

**23.** The fullest study of the case can be found in A.Calder-Marshall, *Lewd, Blasphemous and Obscene*, London, Hutchinson 1972, pp.193ff.

**24.** Quoted in Calder-Marshall, *op. cit.*, p.218.

**25.** Ellis, *Sexual Inversion*, p.352.

**26.** *ibid.*, p.105.

**27.** *ibid.*, p.1, p.325.

**28.** See, for example, D.S.Bailey, *Homosexuality and the Western Christian Tradition*, London, Longman, Green & Co. 1955, p.ix.

**29.** Ellis, *Sexual Inversion*, p.59, pp.82–84, p.301. He noted in a later book, *Psychology of Sex*, London, Heinemann 1946, p.198 that only 8 per cent of observed inverts were 'morbid'!

**30.** *Letters*, Symonds to Edward Carpenter, L.2039, 29 September 1892, and

L.2070, 29 December 1892; Symonds to Ellis, L.1996, 7 July 1892. *Sexual Inversion*, pp.317ff.; *Psychology of Sex*, pp.194ff.

**31.** Edward Carpenter, *The Intermediate Sex*, London, George Allen & Unwin 1908, p.19.

**32.** Ellis, *Sexual Inversion*, p.283.

**33.** *ibid.*, pp.325ff.; and p.338; Ellis, *Psychology of Sex*, pp.212ff.

**34.** Ellis, *Sexual Inversion*, pp.349ff.; p.354.

**35.** Ellis, *Psychology of Sex*, 1946, p.217.

**36.** See for example, Ellis, *Sexual Inversion*, pp.203–204,251,257,258.261. Paul Robinson makes a similar point in his article, cited in 1. above.

**37.** Ellis, *Sexual Inversion*, p.304. For documentation on the relationship between Ellis and Freud, see Vincent Brome, 'Sigmund Freud and Havelock Ellis', *Encounter*, No. 66, March 1959. Ellis's dialogue with Freud can be seen in all the *Studies*, but particularly in the supplementary volume on *Eonism*. See also Ellis, *Psychology of Sex*. This has a restatement of the importance of hormonal differences between the sexes. For Hirschfeld's views on this, which influenced Ellis, see M.Hirschfeld, *Sexual Anomalies and Perversions*, London, Encyclopaedic Press 1952. Freud discusses the connection between bisexuality and inversion in *Three Essays on the Theory of Sexuality*, London, Imago 1949, p.143 (first published 1905). In 1915 he had added a significant footnote which read: 'Psychoanalytical research is most decidedly opposed to any attempt at separating off homosexuals from the rest of mankind as a group of special character.'

**38.** Ellis, *Autoerotism*: *Studies*, vol. 1, part 1, pp.164ff., pp.244–246. See also Robinson, *op. cit.*, p.37.

**39.** Ellis, *Eonism and other Supplementary Studies*: *Studies*, vol. 3, part 2.

**40.** Ellis, *Sex in Relation to Society*: *Studies*, vol. 4, pp.536ff.

**41.** See Ellis, *Love and Pain*, and *Analysis of the Sexual Impulse*: *Studies*, vol. 1, part 2.

**42.** Quoted in *Psychology of Sex*, London, Heinemann 1946, p.287.

**43.** Ellis, *Sex in Relation to Society*, pp.536,577.

**44.** Ellis, *The Sexual Impulse in Women*: *Studies*, vol. 1, part 2, p.189.

**45.** *Studies*, vol. 1, part 2, pp.24,69.

**46.** There is a good discussion of this in Brecher, *op. cit.*

**47.** See Ellis, *Sex in Relation to Society*, p.75; *Man and Woman*, London, Contemporary Science Series, Walter Scott 1894, pp.440,448. There were eight editions of this work up to 1934.

**48.** Ellis, *Sex in Relation to Society*, p.415; *Man and Woman*, pp.447ff.

**49.** Ellis, *Studies*, vol. 3, part 1 (Preface), p.vi; *The Psychic State in Pregnancy*: *Studies*, vol. 3, part 1, p.206; *Sex in Relation to Society*, pp.2–3.

**50.** Ellis, *Sex in Relation to Society*, p.375.

**51.** Ellis, *The Task of Social Hygiene*, p.75.

52. *ibid.*, pp.100ff.

53. Ellis, *Sex in Relation to Society*, p.2, p.32.

54. *ibid.*, p.588, p.20, p.29, p.587.

55. Ellis, *The Task of Social Hygiene*, p.28. A good account of the Eugenics Movement can be found in Linda Gordon, 'The Politics of Population', *Radical America*, vol. 8, No. 4, July–August 1974.

56. See Ellis, 'Women and Socialism', *op. cit.*, p.363.

57. Ellis, *Sex in Relation to Society*, p.582.

58. Linda Gordon, *op. cit.*, pp.72–73.

59. B. Semmel, 'Karl Pearson: Socialist and Darwinist', *British Journal of Sociology*, vol. ix, No. 2, June 1958, p.119, p.122.

60. Quoted in Ellis, *On Life and Sex*, London, Heinemann 1948, p.11.

61. Quotation from Galton from Semmel, *op. cit.*, p.119. References to Key are in Ellis, *Sex in Relation to Society*, pp.580–581.

62. Ellis, *Sex in Relation to Society*, p.586.

63. For details of the general change, see Linda Gordon, *op. cit.*, pp.62ff. For Ellis, see 'The Control of Population' in *More Essays of Love and Virtue*, London, Constable 1931.

64. Ellis, *Psychology of Sex*, p.231. For earlier views, see Ellis, *Sex in Relation to Society*, p.80, pp.363ff.; Ellis, *The Task of Social Hygiene*, p.102. See also 'The Renovation of the Family' in *More Essays of Love and Virtue*. Ellis' dialogue and correspondence with the anthropologist Bronislau Malinowski are key elements in the development of his views on marriage, monogamy and the family.

65. M.D.Young and P.Willmott, *The Symmetrical Family*, London, Institute of Community Studies 1973.

66. Margaret Sanger, *An Autobiography*, London, Victor Gollancz 1939, p.132.

## Select Bibliography

The essays in this book have been based on a wide range of sources, unpublished and published, and this bibliography is not intended to be exhaustive. It gives an indication of the sort of material used, and is also a guide to further reading and research.

There are now a host of books and articles on the period 1880–1914, and in particular the socialist revival of those years, but few manage to illuminate the complex milieu – a mixture of heroic utopianism, sexual millenarianism and hard-headed socialism – from which the politics and ideas of Edward Carpenter and Havelock Ellis developed. A few major biographies manage to capture some of the spirit of the period. The classic study is E.P.Thompson's *William Morris: From Romantic to Revolutionary* (London: Lawrence and Wishart 1955; revised edition, London: Merlin Press 1977). The new edition contains a 'Postscript', published as an article in *New Left Review* 99, which powerfully explores many of the themes which we touch on in this book (completed before the article appeared). Yvonne Kapp's two volumes of *Eleanor Marx* (London: Lawrence and Wishart, vol.1, 1972; vol.2, 1976) offer heroic insights into a socialist who knew both Ellis and Carpenter.

Both this work and Laurence V.Thompson's *The Enthusiasts: Biography of John and Katharine Bruce Glasier* (London: Gollancz 1971) describe the radical change of atmosphere between the 1880s and the late 1890s, early 1900s, which was centrally to affect the nature of the socialism, and the socialists, that were emerging.

Several recent studies of the pioneer socialists of the 1880s offer some of the intellectual flavour. Stanley Pierson's *Marxism and the Origins of British Socialism: the Struggle for a New Consciousness* (Ithaca N.Y.: Cornell University Press 1973) discusses Carpenter's work, and also Ellis in passing. Unfortunately, by concentrating on the ideas, he ignores the movement, and loses sight of essential connections within it. Willard Wolfe, *From Radicalism to Socialism: Men and Ideas in the Formation of Fabian Socialist Doctrines, 1881–1889* (New Haven: Yale University Press 1975) and Norman Mackenzie's book on the early Fabians (forthcoming) deal with the same period.

Gareth Stedman Jones, *Outcast London* (Oxford: Clarendon Press 1971; Harmondsworth: Penguin 1975) discusses the social and economic background of the socialist concepts of the 1880s. The intellectual cross currents, especially relating to the cultural and ethical critique of capitalism, are the central focus of Raymond Williams' classic socialist study, *Culture and Society 1780–1950* (London: Chatto and Windus 1958; Harmondsworth: Penguin 1961, 1963). See also Walter E.Houghton, *The Victorian Frame of Mind* (New Haven: Yale University Press 1957); and Edward Hynes, *The Edwardian Frame of Mind* (Princeton: University Press 1968), which discusses the work of Ellis and Carpenter.

Until recently, most of the many works on the women's movement have tended to ignore that strand of feminism which embraced unconventional sexual ideas. Constance Rover's *Love, Morals and the Feminists* (London: Routledge & Kegan Paul 1970) is a rather staid and cursory glance at its subject, and manages to write off the possibility of a feminist revival on the eve of the birth of the modern women's liberation movement. For a discussion written from within the movement see Sheila Rowbotham, *Hidden from History: 300 Years of Women's Oppression and the Fight against it* (London: Pluto Press 1973). Sheila Rowbotham's *A New World for Women: Stella Browne, Socialist Feminist* (London: Pluto Press 1977) examines the work of a woman on the radical wing of feminism, who was deeply influenced by Ellis and Carpenter.

Ruth First and Ann Scott are preparing a biography of Olive Schreiner, who was closely involved with Ellis and a close friend of Carpenter.

Andrew Rosen, *Rise up Women! The Militant Campaign of the Women's Social and Political Union, 1903–1914* (London: Routledge & Kegan Paul 1974) discusses the more orthodox views of the leading suffragettes, most of whom strongly disapproved of Carpenter and Ellis.

With regard to homosexuality, which concerned both Carpenter and Ellis, little worthwhile has yet been published. The standard work is H. Montgomery Hyde, *The Other Love* (London: Heinemann 1970; London: Mayflower Books [paperback] 1972), which is in the empirical tradition of most studies of homosexuality in history ('great kings and queens'). For an alternative view see Jeffrey Weeks, ' "Sins and Diseases": some notes on homosexuality in the nineteenth century', *History Workshop Journal* No.1, Spring 1976, and Jeffrey Weeks' forthcoming book on homosexual politics in Britain. This latter work attempts to trace the influence of Carpenter and Ellis on later generations of sex reformers.

The sources specifically on Carpenter are now quite varied. Carpenter left a large collection of personal papers, which are now housed with Sheffield City Libraries. The collection includes a great deal of correspondence, as well as a typescript of his memoir of his lover George Merrill, typescripts of some of his works, and press cuttings. John Rylands University Library of Manchester has an early draft of his autobiography, while the Alf Mattison papers (with the Brotherton Library, Leeds University, and Leeds City Libraries) are also relevant.

*A Bibliography of Edward Carpenter* published by Sheffield City Libraries (1949) provides a guide to the collection as well as to his published works. His major works include *Towards Democracy* (first published 1883); *Civilisation: Its Cause and Cure, and Other Essays* (1889); *Love's Coming-of-Age: a series of papers on the relations of the sexes* (1896); *The Intermediate Sex: a Study of some Transitional Types of Men and Women* (1908); *My Days and Dreams: being autobiographical notes* (1916) and *Towards Industrial Freedom* (1917). Most of his books are now out of print, though second hand copies can often be found. *Love's Coming-of-Age* and *The Intermediate Sex* can still be obtained in paperback editions published by George Allen and Unwin.

A discussion of Carpenter's influence can be found in E.M.Forster, *Two Cheers for Democracy* (Harmondsworth: Penguin 1965), though this is not very open about Carpenter's homosexuality. Carpenter's influence on Forster should be illuminated in P.N.Furbank's *E. M. Forster* (vol.1, 1977).

Emile Delavenay, *D. H. Lawrence and Edward Carpenter: A Study in Edwardian Transition* (London: Heinemann 1969) explores a subtle intellectual linkage. Stanley Pierson, 'Edward Carpenter, Prophet of a Socialist Millennium' (*Victorian Studies* vol.13, No.3, March 1970) looks at his socialist vision, but feels compelled to explain his homosexuality in pseudo-scientific terms. Carpenter's local influence is examined in D.K.Barua, 'Edward Carpenter and the Early Sheffield Socialists', *Transactions of the Hunter Archaeological Society*, vol.10, part 1, 1971. D.K.Barua's thesis, cited in the text, is also a useful source. The best brief account of Carpenter is Keith Nield's biography in Joyce Bellamy and John Saville, *Dictionary of Labour Biography* vol.II (London: Macmillan 1975). This has a useful bibliography (pp.91–92).

Havelock Ellis's private papers are less accessible than Carpenter's. They are scattered in various libraries, chiefly in the United States. The University of Texas at Austin has a collection, as do Yale University Library and the University of California, Los Angeles.

The publication history of Ellis's books also tells a more complex story than Carpenter's. His first major works encountered few difficulties: *The New Spirit* (London: G.Bell & Sons 1890); *The Criminal* (London: Walter Scott, Contemporary Science series 1890) and *Man and Woman* (London: Walter Scott 1894). All were re-published in revised editions up to the 1930s. But his major work *Studies in the Psychology of Sex* had a very chequered history. The first volume completed was *Sexual Inversion*. The first edition in English, billed as Volume 1 of the *Studies*, by Havelock Ellis and John Addington Symonds, appeared in 1897 (London: Wilson & Macmillan 1897). After this edition was bought up by Symonds' executor, a second edition, with only Ellis' name on the title page, and with some necessary alterations, appeared in the same year (London and Watford: the University Press). After the court case of 1898 Ellis refused to publish any further parts of the *Studies* in England. The rest of the series (totalling seven volumes in all) was published in the USA, with *Sexual Inversion* now as Volume 2. The short titles of the books were as follows: vol.1, *The Evolution of Modesty*; vol.2, *Sexual Inversion*; vol.3, *Analysis of the Sexual Impulse*; vol.4, *Sexual Selection in Man*; vol.5, *Erotic Symbolism*; vol.6, *Sex in Relation to Society*; vol.7, *Eonism and other Supplementary Studies* (Philadelphia, 1905–10, 1928). This complete series was reissued in 1936, in four volumes, with the parts re-arranged, and with new preliminary matter (New York: Random House 1936). It is this edition that has been used in this book. The volume entitled *Sex in Relation to Society* was published in England in 1937, abridged and revised from the American edition (London: Heinemann 1937).

The best summary of Havelock Ellis's sexual concepts is his *Psychology of Sex* (first published, London: Heinemann 1933). This has gone through a number of impressions and can easily be obtained second hand.

For biographical details, the basic source is Ellis's own *My Life* (first published London and Toronto: Heinemann 1940). A new edition of this, with a foreword by Françoise Delisle, and an introduction and detailed bibliography by Alan Hull Walton, was published in 1967 (London: Spearman 1967). His companion in the last twenty years of his life, Françoise Delisle, published spiritualist memoirs: *Friendship's Odyssey* (London: Heinemann 1946) and *The Return of Havelock Ellis, or Limbo or the Dove* (London: Regency Press 1968). Of many biographies, the best published, despite many inadequacies (including a flip attitude to sexual variations and a Christian bias) is Arthur Calder-Marshall,

*Havelock Ellis* (London: Hart-Davis 1959). The most recent discussion of Ellis's role as a sex reformer is in Paul A.Robinson's *The Modernization of Sex* (London: Elek 1976). Robinson's essay is a good discussion of the central concepts of Ellis's work, but loses a vital dimension by ignoring the cultural milieu in which he wrote. See also E.H.Brecher, *The Sex Researchers* (London: Deutsch 1971). For a discussion of the relationship between Ellis and Freud, see Vincent Brome, 'Sigmund Freud and Havelock Ellis', *Encounter* No.66, March 1959.

# Index

Sheila Rowbotham

# A New World for Women:
## Stella Browne, Socialist Feminist

Stella Browne was one of the few socialists who has dealt openly with the problems presented by sexuality and human reproduction. Born in 1882 in Canada, she became an active worker for socialist feminism in Britain on the eve of the First World War – campaigning for the right to contraception and abortion on demand, asserting women's right to control their own bodies, binding the struggle for sexual liberation with the wider movement for social emancipation. She was a member of the British Communist Party in its first two years and a founder of the Abortion Law Reform Association (ALRA) in 1936. Her insistence on sexual self-determination and her fighting spirit put her at odds with her allies as often as with her enemies. But she was among the most consistent and courageous fighters for socialist feminism. She died in Liverpool in 1955.

Sheila Rowbotham became interested in Stella Browne while writing *Hidden from History*, a study of the changing position of women in England from the puritan revolution to the 1930s, published by Pluto Press. She is a socialist historian and feminist and the author of many books and pamphlets.

Available from bookshops or from
**Pluto Press**
Unit 10 Spencer Court, 7 Chalcot Road,
London NW1 8LH

Sheila Rowbotham

# Hidden from History:
**300 Years of Women's Oppression and
the Fight Against It**
    3rd edition

*Hidden from History* is a study of the changing position of
women in England from the puritan revolution to the 1930s. It
brings together a mass of material on birth control, abortion, and
female sexuality; on the complex relationship of women's
oppression and class exploitation and on the attempts to fuse the
struggles against these two.

It concludes that victory – then and now – depends on 'our
capacity to relate to the working class and the action of working
class women in transforming women's liberation according to their
needs'.

Available from bookshops or from
**Pluto Press**
Unit 10 Spencer Court, 7 Chalcot Road,
London NW1 8LH